In memory of my parents
J. Raymond and Catherine M. Davison
who first taught me to love the scriptures

Contents

Preface

If I were to describe this book in one phrase, I would probably call it a "Bible study on the Bible." The topic is the Bible as a whole—what it is and what it means to us. However, while we will be thinking about the Bible broadly, I will highlight specific passages on a regular basis. The best way to understand the Bible is to become well acquainted with its content. It is one thing to talk about the Bible. It is another thing, of course, to read it with the desire to let its grace-filled words enter our lives.

The Bible is important to all branches of Christendom, but it is especially close to the heart of the Protestant tradition. Reading the Bible has continually been emphasized in the churches issuing from the Reformation. Today, interest in the Bible remains high. It is still a best-seller. Bible studies are written at an accelerating rate. Thousands of people gather weekly in countless congregations to study this special book.

Nevertheless, many people confess that they know little about it, and among large numbers of people—even within our congregations—it often goes unread. What is so special about this book? Why should we care about it? What are we really to believe about it? How are we to understand it, and how can we best read it? We will try to deal with all these questions as we proceed.

Before we begin, however, I want to make two comments related to the contents of this study. First, in case you are unfamiliar with the term "Reformed," you should know that this is one of two main streams that issued from the Reformation in the sixteenth century. The other one is Lutheranism. This latter stream comes of course from Martin Luther, who effectively initiated the Reformation in Germany. The movement for Reformation in Switzerland, which also spread to other countries, such as Scotland and the Netherlands, was somewhat more radical than Luther's version, and it came to be called simply the "Reformed" stream of the larger movement. Presbyterianism is a branch of the Reformed tradition. Other North American churches in the Reformed tradition include the United Church of Christ, the Reformed Church in America, and the United Church of Canada.

In this study, I will be quoting regularly from official confessions of the Reformation churches. The Presbyterian Church (U.S.A.) is guided by eleven confessional documents. These are printed as Part I: *Book of Confessions* of *The Constitution of the Presbyterian Church (U.S.A.)*. Where they are cited in the text, I will give the usual references to the sections of the document; however, since the referencing system within the *Book of Confessions* is especially helpful, I will include that information in parentheses too. For instance, a citation of the third paragraph of the first chapter of the Second Helvetic Confession would look like this: I (5.003).

Second, I want to express some notes of gratitude. The overall conception for this study arose as I taught a class of dedicated (and probably long-suffering) members of Westminster Presbyterian Church in Upper St. Clair, a suburb of Pittsburgh, Pennsylvania. The Monday Bible Study has been meeting for years, and we have covered many topics together. The "first draft" of this book, so to speak, came out of our study together. I am grateful to each of the members of the class for their insights and ideas—and for their love of scripture. My thanks also go to Gail King and Sandy Conley, friends and colleagues at Westminster, for their comments and suggestions on the manuscript. I am especially grateful to my wife, Reeny, who has supported me and encouraged me strongly even in the midst of her own very busy schedule. Thanks be to God, whose words are a lamp to our feet and a light to our paths (Ps. 119:105).

James E. Davison
Lent 2001

Introduction

A Holy Book

When you think of the Bible, what is your first thought? Probably you think of a book. Perhaps you picture it lying on a pulpit or resting on a desk or table. At one time, you would certainly have imagined it with a black cover, but nowadays Bibles come in many colors. They come in many shapes and sizes too. In fact, the Bible can be purchased in so many different formats that your image of what the Bible looks like may be a bit blurred.

In the tradition of the Reformation, the Bible has always been a cherished book. People have relied on the scriptures for support, comfort, and hope. The very names used for the Bible attest to its incredible importance in Protestant communities ever since the earliest days of the Reformation. "Bible," first of all, derives from a Greek word for "book." The fact that it is often called *the* book is an indication of its supreme importance and ultimate authority in the Christian faith. The other term, "scripture" or "the scriptures," derives from a Latin word meaning "writing." The implication of this term is that the Bible is *the* writing par excellence. In this book, I will use the terms interchangeably.

You have probably noticed that the marketing world has latched onto this term. Sometimes "bible" is used in the title of a publication to indicate that it is the standard volume on a subject or the most significant handbook in a given field. For instance, a book might be called *The Fisherman's Bible* or *The Bible for Birdwatchers.* Indirectly, this application of the word testifies to how important the Bible is perceived to be by the general public.

> "For many people these days, the Bible is a closed book."

In spite of these powerful names, however, for many people these days, the Bible is in fact a closed book. The number of people who read the scriptures regularly has declined, as has the number of people who read it occasionally. Even those of us who have been brought up on the Bible may find that it seems like a strange book to us. It is, after all, a terribly ancient book. As I write this introduction, I hear a passenger jet flying overhead. This past week, the news media reported on yet another interplanetary mission. Advances in biotechnology and information technology move forward at a relentless pace. Each day, the world of our ancestors seems to recede further and further into the past. Why, then, should we read an ancient book?

Yet, even when the Bible goes unread, and in spite of the fact that it presupposes a world that is light years removed from our own, something in us senses that the Bible is special. It is not quite like other books. It is more significant than other written works. It deserves our attention and it ought to be read. I have heard many people express regrets that they have not read from the scriptures very often. They feel that they have missed something, and they are vaguely disappointed with themselves for not making Bible reading more of a priority in their lives.

Part of the problem is that many people are uncertain what to make of this book called the Bible. What kind of book is it? What do we believe about it and what should we expect to find in it? How can we approach the Bible beneficially, so that we will be blessed rather than frustrated in our reading? These are the kinds of questions that we will deal with in this study. We will attempt to understand the character as well as the characteristics of this unique book. Throughout, we will try to grasp the role it plays in our striving to be faithful to Jesus Christ in this world—as different as it may be from the world of the Bible itself.

The Power of Words

One of the first things we need to recognize about the Bible is that it came from a primarily oral culture. Israel's great statement of faith, the Shema, is taken from Deuteronomy 6:4. It begins with the words, "Hear, O Israel: The LORD is our God, the LORD alone." The words of the Law may be written down, but for the vast majority of people the issue is to *hear* those words as they are recited.

In modern societies like ours, it is common to devalue the significance of words. "It's just words" is not an uncommon statement. For the ancient Israelites, in contrast, words were a potent force. They anticipated that words could have an enormous effect for good or ill. H. Wheeler Robinson quotes a classic story that illustrates the power of words well. It seems that a Middle Eastern father and his son met an enemy, whereupon "the father threw his boy on the ground so that the enemy's curses might pass over his head without harming him; he treated the curses, in fact, just like the blast of a bomb."

Words are powerful forces. They can help you or harm you. They can heal you or damage you. As you might anticipate, this is why formal blessings and curses are so significant in the Bible. To speak a word of blessing is to bring something good into a person's life. To curse that person is to cause harm to him or her in a tangible way.

To see how seriously the Israelites took blessings, we only need to recall the story of Jacob's deception of his father, Isaac. Genesis 27 relates the sad tale. Esau is the older of the twin brothers, and he is the one who, according to the traditions of the culture, should be the recipient of the blessing. Isaac calls Esau to his side and asks him to hunt game and prepare a meal, at which time Isaac will give his son the blessing. While Esau is in the field, Jacob—aided by his mother, Rebekah—prepares a meal and dresses himself in a manner calculated to deceive his father's failing senses. When Jacob brings the meal to Isaac, the old man is suspicious, but he falls victim to the deceit. Solemnly, Isaac blesses the wrong son: "May God give you of the dew of heaven, and of the fatness of the

> "The word of God is living and active, sharper than any two-edged sword."
> (Hebrews 4:12)

earth, . . . Be lord over your brothers, . . . Cursed be everyone who curses you, and blessed be everyone who blesses you!" (Gen. 27:28–29).

The very blessing pronounced over Jacob gives him precedence over his brother, who is the rightful heir. We might say, "Take it back!" Yet as we read further in this disturbing story, we discover that the blessing cannot be taken back. When Isaac learns the truth, he cries out in anguish: "Who was it then that hunted game and brought it to me, . . . and I have blessed him?—yes, and blessed he shall be!" (v. 33).

Even words spoken erroneously carry out their effect. The dynamism in words is also the background for the declaration in Isaiah 55:10–11:

> For as the rain and the snow come down from heaven,
>   and do not return there until they have watered the earth,
> making it bring forth and sprout,
>   giving seed to the sower and bread to the eater,
> so shall my word be that goes out from my mouth;
>   it shall not return to me empty,
> but it shall accomplish that which I purpose,
>   and succeed in the thing for which I sent it.

This may remind you of the description of creation in Genesis 1, where the introduction to each of the segments of the created order is simply, "And God said, 'Let there be.'" The following refrain is, "And it was so." God's very speaking of the words brings forth the realities. Words spoken by human beings carry great power; words spoken by God are incredibly potent.

We can find the same respect for the potency of God's Word in the New Testament. The letter to the Hebrews includes the assertion, "the word of God is living and active, sharper than any two-edged sword, piercing until it divides soul from spirit, joints from marrow; it is able to judge the thoughts and intentions of the heart" (Heb. 4:12). This assertion comes in the context of a series of quotations from the Old Testament that warn against the danger of unfaithfulness to God. These passages are quite capable of executing the vindication or judgment they speak of, says the writer.

The Holiness of Written Words

Words carry great power. It should not be surprising then that the words written in books receive special reverence. In ancient times, books were uncommon. As we shall see later, producing them was a time-consuming and laborious process, and the number of people who could read them was limited. Precisely because they were so uncommon, books were treasured. More than that, they were revered. They seemed to be mysterious and profound. If words by their very nature seemed to be dynamic and potent, then words inscribed in a book conveyed an even higher level of certainty as well as validity.

Think of the Ten Commandments for a moment. Not only are these decrees from God, but they are written on stone tablets: "When God finished speaking with Moses on Mount Sinai, he gave him the two tablets of the covenant, tablets of stone, written with the finger of God" (Ex. 31:18). The commandments are firm and final. Nothing can undermine or cancel their validity. This event, in a sense, becomes the model for what happens in later Israelite history. When a highly important pronouncement is to be made,

"Write in a book all the words that I have spoken to you." (Jeremiah 30:1)

it is put into writing. The words are not chiseled into stone tablets, but inscribing them into a book provides a similar testimony to their significance.

The prophet Jeremiah offers an example of this. In chapter 30, a word comes to him from God:

> Thus says the LORD, the God of Israel: Write in a book all the words that I have spoken to you. For the days are surely coming, says the LORD, when I will restore the fortunes of my people, Israel and Judah, says the LORD, and I will bring them back to the land that I gave to their ancestors and they shall take possession of it. (Jer. 30:1–3)

It may seem inconceivable that Israel and Judah could be restored following total destruction, but God's promise is secure, for it has been written in a book!

You can see the same theme at work in the context of final judgment. Daniel 7:9–10 offers an arresting vision of the last day. Daniel sees "an Ancient One" taking his place on a throne. His appearance is splendid; his power and glory are awesome; and he is attended by a staggering number of servants. Then we read, "The court sat in judgment, and the books were opened." It is obvious that what stands in the books is what will be decisive in the judgment.

At the end of Daniel, there is a similar assumption of the certainty of written words, but this time the book in which they are written is closed to view. In Daniel 12:1–4, toward the end of an extended visionary pronouncement to Daniel describing the end times, we read that the archangel Michael will come forth in a period of tremendous calamity. The people of Israel, however, will be spared. They are described as "everyone who is found written in the book." Further, Daniel is instructed to "keep the words secret and the book sealed until the time of the end." You can clearly perceive the underlying assumption that, because these words are inscribed in a book, they have a force to them that cannot be annulled. At the proper time, what these words proclaim will surely, inexorably take place.

We can also find these themes—the certainty of written words and the safeguarding of those whose names are written in a heavenly book—in the book of Revelation in the New Testament. For example, to begin with the second of these themes, chapter 13 describes a ferocious beast, and then announces that this creature will exercise power over all those "whose name has not been written from the foundation of the world in the book of life of the Lamb that was slaughtered" (Rev. 13:8). The book contains a list of those whom God will preserve. Notice that the list is so firm that it was put in writing already before the world was made.

> "Rejoice that your names are written in heaven."
> (Luke 10:20)

As a matter of fact, this picture of names inscribed in a book is rather common in both the Old and New Testaments. There is an interesting episode in Exodus at the time the Israelites make the golden calf at the foot of Mount Sinai. Moses intercedes with God on behalf of the people, asking for their forgiveness. Then he prays that, if the Lord will not forgive, then "blot me out of the book that you have written" (Ex. 32:32). The same phrase can be found in Psalm 69, where the anguish and suffering of the writer cause him to wish that those who seek to harm him will "be blotted out of the book of the living" (Ps. 69:28).

The same image of names in books appears in a number of other places in the New Testament. Jesus says at one point, "Rejoice that your names are written in heaven" (Luke 10:20). Paul, in his letter to the Philippians, mentions some of his coworkers and comments that their "names are in the book of life" (Phil. 4:3). Also, the letter to the Hebrews refers to those "who are enrolled in heaven" (Heb. 12:23).

Returning to the book of Revelation, notice the other theme of the certainty of words inscribed in a book. Chapter 4 introduces a vision of the glories of heaven and worship of almighty God. Then as chapter 5 opens, we see that the One on the throne is holding a scroll that is sealed with seven seals. Very solemnly we are told that no one on earth or in heaven is able to open this scroll, except "the Lion of the tribe of Judah" (Rev. 5:2–5). As we read on in Revelation, we see the staggering effects that occur each time a seal is opened. As the seventh seal is finally removed in chapter 8, even more apocalyptic events unfold. Clearly, what stands written in this book happens as it has been recorded.

If words carry so much potency, and if words written in a book produce such irresistible results, you can imagine how greatly books were revered. Ancient peoples stood in awe of books. There was a sense of veneration for religious books, in particular, for they were felt to be holy. It is not surprising that, in Christian history, the Bible came to be called the *Holy Bible.*

Scripture in Today's World

In light of what we have been discussing, we can indicate two obvious problems related to the Bible. Simply put, words are not powerful and books are not holy anymore. It will not require much reflection to see the truth of each of these points. Words convey little power, simply because they are so abundant. In contemporary culture, we are surrounded by words. Turn on your radio, choose a channel on the television, enter an airport terminal, or visit a shopping mall. Everywhere you go, you will hear a cacophony of words striving to capture your attention. The effect is that we may feel almost verbally assaulted by all the clamor for our attention. As a result, we sometimes pay only partial attention. Occasionally we don't listen at all. Compare that to the belief in ancient times that words could bless or curse you.

> In the contemporary world, words are not powerful and books are not holy.

If words have lost their power, it is not surprising that books are no longer holy. Just as so many words are spoken, incredible numbers of words are written. Print runs of a given book can go into the millions, and thousands of books are published annually. In addition, there are innumerable magazines and newspapers producing millions of words—not to mention newsletters, legal contracts, mass mailings, and, of course, Christmas letters. The amount of material that appears in print is simply astounding.

The printed word, consequently, carries very little weight. Whereas ancient readers pondered books, modern readers take a consumer approach to reading. Books are a way of picking up information quickly, or books allow us to escape for a while into another world. When a novel is especially exciting and suspenseful, we call it a "page turner." We do not pause to think much about anything we read in the novel; the words just go by very quickly. No longer rare, books have become not just commonplace but disposable as well. The result is that books, which held a place of high authority in antiquity, are now things to be used and then discarded without a second thought.

The implications of all of this for the scriptures should be obvious. There is not as much holiness attached to the "Holy Bible" any longer. As a youth, I remember hearing an adult remark that, if you placed a Bible in a stack with a number of other books, you should always be certain to place the Bible on top. As odd as that comment may seem to some of us, at least there was some sense in it that the Bible is special. It ought to be treated differently from other books. These days, this sense has receded further from view.

As I mentioned above, Bibles come in many different formats. Just like other products in our consumer-oriented society, Bibles are produced for particular niches of the market. There is a danger with this approach, however. When you no longer feel part of that niche, it could be easy to assume that there is no relevance any longer to this particular version—or worse, to any version—of the Bible. Another danger is more general. The Bible can easily be treated as a source for gaining some desirable information. Then, when it has been read, it can be laid aside or placed on a shelf along with a variety of other books that are no longer needed.

"Ignorance of the Scriptures is a precipice and a deep abyss." (Epiphanius, Bishop of Cyprus)

These tendencies in our culture fly in the face of our confession about the significance of this book. In the Christian church, we confess that the Bible is not simply one book among all the rest. It is unique and it is authoritative. The nature of scripture is stifled if it is treated as so many other books are. The Bible is not a "page turner" or a "thriller." It is not designed like a book that provides how-to information, such as a diet plan or a computer manual. Scripture will not reveal its secrets if it is treated as a "quick read." Rather, we have to spend time with this book. We need to read it reflectively, asking what its stories and admonitions and poetry and aphorisms have to say to our spirits.

Reading the Bible as it is designed demands time and attention. It requires not just reading but rereading. As we interact with the book over extended periods of time, scripture unlocks its riches more and more fully. Gradually we reach the point where we can say with the psalmist, "How sweet are your words to my taste, sweeter than honey to my mouth!" (Ps. 119:103). The goal of Bible reading is to extract that sort of sweetness from its words—to uncover truths that are sometimes comforting and soothing, sometimes disturbing and unsettling, but always beneficial and profitable for our lives.

This book is intended to help you understand better how to look at the scriptures so that you will know better how to use them. The goal is not to present study methods, since a host of other books can provide that. Instead, the goal will be to look at what the Bible as a whole is all about. What is it that sets the Bible apart? Why is it holy? Why is it important—even necessary—to approach the Bible differently from other books? My hope is that, by considering what kind of book the Bible is, we will understand better what to expect from it and how to interact with it. Most significantly, we will gain a sense of how to open ourselves to allow God's Spirit to speak through its pages to our hearts in ways that will make it truly a "book of life" for all the days of our lives.

Questions for Reflection

- What is your first thought when you hear the words, "the Bible"? Are there memories that you associate with the scriptures from your youth or childhood? If so, how would you compare them to your understanding of the Bible at this stage in your life?

- What has been your experience in reading the Bible? Is it an "open" or a "closed" book for you? As you begin reading this study, how important do you think reading regularly from the scriptures is for our growth in the Christian life?

- Are there portions of the Bible that you like especially? Reflect on what attracts you to those particular biblical passages.

PART I   The Divine Word in Book Form

Chapter 1

How the Bible Came Together

This particular book that we call the Bible is really a collection of many books. There are sixty-six in all, at least by the count of most Protestant denominations. Not only does the Bible contain a large number of books, but—as we will notice shortly—there are also many different kinds of writings included between the covers of the Bible. Have you ever wondered how all those writings came together as one book?

Somehow we are inclined to think that the Bible has always been this way. A friend was talking about his aged grandmother some time ago. She had emigrated from Germany, and he remembered her clear sentiment that the King James Version was just not quite "the real Bible." For her, as you might guess, the true Bible was the "Luther Bible," that is, the German translation that went back to Martin Luther in the sixteenth century!

If we stop to think about it, it is obvious that the Bible has not always been the way we know it. It did not simply drop out of heaven, so to speak, directly into our hands. Rather, the Bible has existed in a variety of forms, and it has come down to us through the centuries via a long, complex process. In this chapter, we will be looking at the primary elements in the process that made it possible for us to possess a Bible—of whatever color, shape, and size.

Composing the Biblical Writings

Within the Bible itself, we can find descriptions of the process of composition that resulted in some of the writings. Jeremiah, the famous prophet who lived in Jerusalem around 600 B.C., provides one of the most interesting accounts. Chapter 36 of the book of Jeremiah tells the story. At God's command, the prophet dictates a writing that records the Lord's judgments on the people for their sins and disobedience. Baruch, Jeremiah's secretary, records the words in a scroll. Then Jeremiah sends Baruch to read the scroll in the Temple in hopes of awakening the consciences of the people.

Some of the governmental officials are indeed impressed. They propose to take the scroll to Jehoiakim, the king. Wisely, they also tell both Baruch and Jeremiah to go into hiding. One of the king's officers, Jehudi, carries the scroll to the king. We get a rather picturesque description of what follows: "Now the king was sitting in his winter apartment . . . and there was a fire burning in the brazier before him. As Jehudi read three or four columns, the king would cut them off with a penknife and throw them into the fire in the brazier, until the entire scroll was consumed" (Jer. 36:22–23). Afterward, in response to the king's obstinacy, God simply commands Jeremiah to dictate another scroll with the same message!

This scroll, or large parts of it at least, end up in the book we know as Jeremiah. In passing, we should note that the book of Jeremiah as a whole would also have been written on a scroll. We will return to this in more detail shortly. Jeremiah appears to be assembled out of various speeches and writings from Jeremiah's ministry. Other events are recorded too. Some of them are as dramatic as the one just mentioned. Since the book of Jeremiah does not seem to follow any particular order—by chronology or by theme, for instance—it is especially hard for us as modern readers to understand the settings in which the prophetic messages were delivered. Thus, many times it is also hard to understand their meaning.

In general, it appears that the books of the Hebrew prophets were put together in what seems to us to be a somewhat haphazard manner. The ministries of the prophets were primarily oral: they proclaimed the "word of the Lord" to the people in particular situations, often at risk to their lives. Because those words were so significant, they—or their disciples—would record them. Over time, they compiled the words of the prophet into a larger collection. Usually, the compilation would not follow any careful organization, at least according to our standards. Often, it is hard for us to follow the line of thought in the writings of the prophets. However, even if the manner of organizing the material is somewhat random, at least their messages have been preserved for later generations.

We encounter a different kind of composition in the writings that document the history of Israel. The books of the Kings and the Chronicles offer a running narrative of the people of Israel, first as a united kingdom under Saul, David, and Solomon, and then as a divided kingdom—Israel and Judah—under the remaining kings. Organized around the reigns of the kings, and moving back and forth between Israel's and Judah's rulers, the story follows the progress of both North (Israel) and South (Judah) as each moves, seemingly inevitably, to destruction and ruin by the great empires.

Famous figures dominate the narratives. We read about kings such as Ahab,

Hezekiah, and Josiah, or prophets such as Elijah and Elisha. But these chroniclers are intent on recording accurately all of the kings in both Israel and Judah. Thus, we hear about Pekahiah, who began to reign in the Northern Kingdom at the death of his father Menahem. There is not much to say about Pekahiah, except that "he did what was evil in the sight of the LORD" (2 Kings 15:24). Though he only reigned two years before dying in a revolt, in one sense Pekahiah did pretty well. Earlier in this same chapter the writer reports on two other kings in the Northern Kingdom, Zechariah and Shallum. They are noteworthy primarily because they ruled for six months and one month, respectively (15:8,13).

> "Shallum the son of Jabesh began to reign in the thirty-ninth year of Uzziah king of Judah, and he reigned one month in Samaria."
> (2 Kings 15:13)

In these histories of the kings, it is interesting that the writers so readily highlight not only the successes and achievements but especially the foibles and failures of the kings. Since these writers were from the educated class, they were closely connected to the royal courts. In some cases they may have been in their employ. Often in traditional societies, chronicles of the rulers are cleansed and sanitized. Rulers do not seem to want to hear that royalty—even their predecessors from other lines of descent—could be less than exemplary figures. So the lists are often just that—lists. Here, however, we find that many of the rulers are judged negatively; they are wicked, even depraved. We should note too, though, that there is also a simplicity to these records. Very little "gray" enters into judgments on the various kings. Either they do what is right in the sight of the Lord, or they do what is evil in the sight of the Lord.

How, then, were these books in the Bible composed? The short answer is: in a painstaking, careful way. The difference between this kind of composition and the almost stream-of-consciousness kind of writing that we encounter in the prophets will be obvious when you read one sort of writing after the other. The Old Testament has not come to be by means of one method of composition. Various techniques of composition are the rule rather than the exception.

To experience the same kind of contrast in the New Testament, compare for a moment the Gospels and Paul's letters. Let's begin with the Gospel of Luke. We can gain an idea of what was going on in the mind of the author of this Gospel from its opening words:

> Since many have undertaken to set down an orderly account of the events that have been fulfilled among us, . . . I too decided, after investigating everything carefully from the very first, to write an orderly account

for you, most excellent Theophilus, so that you may know the truth concerning the things about which you have been instructed. (Luke 1:1–4)

In passing, you may be curious who "Theophilus," the recipient of this Gospel, was. Scholars wonder about this too. Since the name means "friend of God," some think that the name is intended to apply to all readers. Most, however, believe that the Gospel of Luke is indeed addressed to an individual person, possibly the patron who underwrote Luke's work. In either case, notice how the author of the Gospel describes his own work in composing this account of the life of Jesus Christ. Not only did he work hard to collect the materials, but he also sought to verify carefully their accuracy.

Another Gospel also provides a hint about its composition. The Gospel of John contains this comment near the end of the book: "Now Jesus did many other signs in the presence of his disciples, which are not written in this book. But these are written so that you may come to believe that Jesus is the Messiah, the Son of God, and that through believing you may have life in his name" (John 20:30–31).

As with the Gospel of Luke, this description portrays an author sitting and reflecting. "How can I best structure my narrative of Jesus' life?" "Which stories, events, and sayings are most important to include?" You can almost feel the quiet, earnest deliberations going on in their minds as these writers piece together the story of Jesus Christ for the sake of their readers.

"Yet the Bible was composed in such a way that as beginners mature, its meaning grows with them." (St. Augustine, *Confessions*)

Compare this calm, deliberative method to Paul's approach. In some of his letters he is anxious and alarmed, even angry, at the actions of the congregations reported to him. For instance, Paul hears that the Christians at Galatia are being enticed by Judaizing missionaries to adopt the requirements of Jewish law in addition to trusting in Jesus Christ. At the beginning of his letter to the Galatians, Paul opens with an expression of deep disappointment: "I am astonished that you are so quickly deserting the one who called you in the grace of Christ and are turning to a different gospel" (Gal. 1:6). A little later in the same letter he bursts out, "You foolish Galatians! Who has bewitched you?" (3:1).

Another congregation, where Paul had expended much effort, creates problems for him when members begin to disparage his work. Paul writes to these Christians to remind them of how much he has sacrificed for his ministry:

This is my defense to those who would examine me. Do we not have the right to our food and drink? Do we not have the right to be accompanied by a believing wife, as do the other apostles and the brothers of the Lord and Cephas? Or is it only Barnabas and I who have no right to refrain from working for a living? (1 Cor. 9:3–6)

We can take a final example from later in Paul's ministry. He has been imprisoned and is well aware that his imprisonment could easily lead to his execution. Paul confesses some of his anxieties and expectations to the Philippians, a group with whom he seems to have a particularly close and affectionate bond. Near the beginning of his letter, he expresses the hope that his manner of life will glorify Christ, whether he lives or dies. Then he continues:

For to me, living is Christ and dying is gain. If I am to live in the flesh, that means fruitful labor for me; and I do not know which I prefer. I am hard pressed between the two: my desire is to depart and be with Christ, for that is far better; but to remain in the flesh is more necessary for you. (Phil. 1:21–24)

These examples are good indications of how much of what Paul communicates is due not only to the situation in the congregation he is addressing, but also to his own circumstances at the time of writing. For this reason, the epistles of Paul are often called "occasional" letters. They are written in a specific situation for a particular purpose to a special group of people. Only in the letter to the Romans does Paul provide something of a theological essay on his understanding of the gospel. Otherwise, the letters—not only of Paul but also of other writers in the New Testament—do not offer general discussions of beliefs or ethics intended for a broad audience. That is one reason why such different interpretations are possible within our churches regarding doctrinal and moral issues. I will speak more on this in chapters 6 and 7. The point here is simply to recognize that careful study is necessary to determine what a discussion in a biblical writing, aimed at a specific group, might imply for our own situation. After all, our culture seems to be light-years away from the biblical world.

> The epistles of Paul are written in a specific situation for a particular purpose to a special group of people.

These are but a few examples of the different kinds of literature that make up the Old and New Testaments. The whole process by which the biblical books were composed was highly involved and intricate. The same can be said with respect to the manner in which these many individual writings were eventually brought into one book—our Bible.

Collecting the Biblical Writings

The process of writing books of the Bible, as we have just seen, followed many different patterns and took place in many different locations and time periods. You can readily guess that bringing the various writings together must have been an equally complex process. How did we get *one* book from these *many* books? How were the biblical writings collected?

We can get at this topic by noticing that some of the biblical books were themselves put together as a collection of materials. Look at the Psalms, for instance. If you read the heading just prior to the first psalm, you will see an interesting title: Book I. This title covers the first forty-one psalms. You will not be surprised to hear, therefore, that the entire book of Psalms is actually composed of a number of books. There are five in all. Within each of these books a number of psalms have been brought together. The reasons why particular psalms have been associated with each other appear to be rather undefined. Sometimes a group of psalms belongs to the same literary type. At other times, the name of a guild of musicians, such as Korah or Asaph, is attached to the titles. The particular name used for God—Yahweh or Elohim—can even serve as a principle of joining psalms. For this reason, the Psalms have sometimes been called a "collection of collections."

We saw earlier that the book of Jeremiah was assembled from the many individual records of his prophecies. This would appear to be the case with most of the prophets. Certainly, it is true of those whose careers extended over longer periods of time. An obvious illustration is Isaiah, who appears to have been active for about forty years, during the reigns of four kings (Isa. 1:1). Scholars commonly hold that this book offers more than a collection only of Isaiah's words over that lengthy period of time. Rather, the great differences in literary style, historical setting, and theological themes from chapter 40 onward suggest that at least one and possibly two additional authors (or groups of authors) added further sections to the work. The names sometimes used to designate these additional divisions are not particularly creative: Second Isaiah (chapters 40—55) and Third Isaiah (chapters 56—66). The names are not inappropriate, however, for they help to bring out the fact that, if these are indeed additions to the original work, they were composed by disciples of Isaiah, who continued to prophesy in his tradition, speaking to new and different situations in his name.

We could illustrate this process of collecting individual writings easily with the New Testament documents as well. For example, the Synoptic Gospels—Matthew, Mark, and Luke—are obviously closely connected with one another. It is generally assumed that Mark was written first. The authors of both Matthew and Luke had access to Mark and used it in composing their Gospels. It would appear that they both made use of another source, which is no longer available. That source is normally called "Q," and it seems to have contained a collection of Jesus' sayings. In addition to these two sources that they used in common, Matthew and Luke consulted other sources that were available to them.

The Synoptic Gospels, then, also bear the marks of being a collection of materials. The same could be shown for the Gospel of John and for a number of the letters of Paul. On one level, the writings within the Bible were often compiled by collecting individual materials and joining them into a larger whole. On another level, these writings were gradually brought together into more complete collections. The determining factor was the belief that these particular works were holy. They reflected God's words and will for the people. It was because they were recognized to be such significant books that they were preserved and protected.

> The determining factor in collecting biblical books was the belief that these particular works were holy, reflecting God's words and will for the people.

Much of this process must have been somewhat haphazard. Remember that the "books" we are speaking of in Old and New Testament times were written primarily in the form of scrolls. Each scroll could contain one or more writing, depending on two factors: the lengths of the books and the size of the scroll. You may be familiar with the Isaiah Scroll found among the Dead Sea Scrolls, which came from the Essene sect at the desert monastery of Qumran. Qumran was destroyed by the Romans prior to the destruction of Jerusalem in A.D. 70 and the famous siege at Masada that ended in A.D. 73.

Along with many other writings, the Isaiah Scroll was hidden away in the desert, only to be rediscovered in 1947. A facsimile of the scroll is on display in the Shrine of the Book in Jerusalem. It is about as lengthy as a scroll was normally made, stretching to nearly twenty-four feet in length. Scrolls could be larger, but they became increasingly unwieldy as the length increased. In fact, scrolls were usually shorter than the Isaiah Scroll. A scroll might be used to contain one writing, but oftentimes a scroll might consist of multiple writings. All twelve of the minor prophets, for example, can fit into one scroll.

As scrolls were collected, you can imagine them being matched with others of the same kind—wisdom literature or prophetic writings, for instance.

The arrangement would be somewhat fluid, and there would have been little apprehension that some writings come "before" or "after" others. That sense expands only at a later time, when the writings are arranged in book form.

There is a curious account in 2 Kings that will illustrate some of the fluidity inherent in books in ancient times. In chapter 22, we read about Josiah's reign in Jerusalem. He determines to have the "house of the LORD" repaired. In the process of assessing the condition of the temple, the high priest makes what seems like a very odd discovery: "I have found the book of the law in the house of the LORD" (2 Kings 22:8). When the king learns of this discovery, he tears his clothes in a sign of remorse and leads the people in restoring their commitment to follow the laws of God: "The king stood by the pillar and made a covenant before the LORD, to follow the LORD, keeping his commandments, his decrees, and his statutes, with all his heart and all his soul, to perform the words of this covenant that were written in this book. All the people joined in the covenant" (23:3).

> "I have found the book of the law in the house of the LORD." (2 Kings 22:8)

Then the people celebrate their renewed faithfulness by keeping the Passover. Precisely what this "book of the law" was is unclear. Most scholars assume that it is connected in some way to our present book of Deuteronomy.

Be that as it may, this somewhat odd story can serve as a reminder that, in a largely oral society where scrolls are rare, it would be relatively easy for a writing to fall into disuse.

It is probably obvious that in this kind of society, the idea of a "list" of holy books was scarcely operative. Over time, scrolls were collected, especially in appropriate groupings. Thus, what we have come to call the Hebrew Scriptures, or the Old Testament, was created gradually out of scrolls containing books of the law, historical books, wisdom literature, and prophetic books. By the time of Jesus, these groupings (and the specific writings included in them) were basically in place.

In the New Testament, therefore, we find Jesus speaking of "the law and the prophets" as a commonly recognized unit. "Do not think that I have come to abolish the law or the prophets," he says in one place (Matt. 5:17). Or notice the parable of the rich man and Lazarus. When the rich man, following his death, finds himself in torment in Hades, he calls out to Father Abraham to warn his five brothers about his agony. Jesus puts these words on the lips of Abraham: "They have Moses and the prophets; they should listen to them" (Luke 16:29).

Still, precisely which books were God's holy writings remained somewhat disputed. Even following Jesus' ministry, the rabbis continued to discuss whether a few of the writings truly belonged in the canon. We will come back to this in the next section. For now, it is sufficient to note that, even at the time of Jesus, the boundaries of the Old Testament remained somewhat in flux.

What we have seen with the Old Testament is mirrored in the New Testament. Writings were composed individually for specific purposes, but as people realized their general value, they were copied and circulated for wider audiences. To see one way this worked, notice the letters of Paul. The apostle Paul wrote his letters to particular local congregations to discuss crucial issues in the lives of those earliest Christians. Sometimes those discussions were more like debates. You might skim through 1 Corinthians or Galatians to look for signs of these controversies. It will not take long for you to picture how intense the issues were.

Even though Paul had in mind particular groups of Christians when he wrote his letters, we can easily imagine that members in other Pauline congregations would be very much interested in what he had written. When they learned that Paul had composed a letter to such and such a church, they would likely try to get hold of a copy of what he had to say. Especially in the larger metropolitan areas, such as Rome, there was strong interest in collecting copies of all the letters that went by Paul's name.

The earliest collection of New Testament writings may well have been Paul's letters. As an aside, it may be that collecting Paul's writings provided the impetus for Christian communities to move from the scroll to the codex form of books. Codexes, constructed similarly to our modern books, were well known but were usually reserved for providing information on pragmatic subjects. True books in the ancient world were scrolls. However, in Christian circles, the codex rapidly became the form used for all scriptural texts. Because the leaves of codexes permitted writing on both sides, the codex was less expensive than the scroll. Codexes were also easier to open and to use for reference purposes. It was their use in the Christian movement that led codexes to displace scrolls in the third and fourth centuries. It may well have been the use of the codex already to collect Paul's writings that provided the initial thrust in this direction.[1]

Codex: a Latin word referring to the first books, which were made from sheets of wood, covered with wax. Later, papyrus and parchment were used for the pages of the codex.

As with the Old Testament, groups of new books were collected gradually. Over time, the larger units were brought together. Also like the Old Testament, the precise collection remained fluid for some time. How then did these collections get into final form? This question leads us to the final section of this chapter.

Canonizing the Biblical Writings

It is one thing to bring the many biblical writings together. It is quite another to know that all of the books really belong together. After asking how we got many books into one, we also need to ask a further question. How do we know that we have the *right* books in the final collection?[2]

This is what is called the question of canon. The word means "standard," "rule," or "norm." It suggests the idea of a criterion by which doctrinal and ethical viewpoints can be gauged. The word canon has become a technical term for the group of inspired books that make up Holy Scripture and serve as the norm for faith and life in the church.

To get at the issues here, let's look at a specific case. Consider this problem: Does the letter to the Hebrews belong in scripture? Certainly, we find it in our Bibles today. Early on, however, there were doubts about whether it should be considered to be inspired or not. The book presents a wondrous picture of Jesus Christ as our "great high priest who has passed through the heavens," who can "sympathize with our weaknesses," and because of whom we can "approach the throne of grace with boldness, so that we may receive mercy and find grace to help in time of need" (Heb. 4:14–16).

Nestled in the text, though, are disconcerting references to limitations on God's willingness to forgive those who fall away from the faith. The language sounds not simply forthright, but harsh:

> For it is impossible to restore again to repentance those who have once been enlightened, and have tasted the heavenly gift, and have shared in the Holy Spirit, and have tasted the goodness of the word of God and the powers of the age to come, and then have fallen away, since on their own they are crucifying again the Son of God and are holding him up to contempt. (6:4–6)

How can such a statement be reconciled with the many promises of overwhelming mercy and unlimited forgiveness that we hear often enough from the lips of Jesus? When Peter asks Jesus in Matthew how often he should be willing to forgive, implying that seven times should be more than sufficient, Jesus replies, "Not seven times, but, I tell you, seventy-seven times" (Matt. 18:22).

In assessing the content of Hebrews, we need to bear in mind the purpose of the writing. Really something of a sermon, the book is admonishing people to remain faithful to Jesus Christ in spite of the risk of persecution. The author wants to underline the serious nature of apostasy in the face of the threats of physical harm. To deny Jesus Christ, who gave his life for you, says the author, would be a grave offense against the grace you have received from God. To some extent, then, the severity of the language is due to the seriousness of the situation.

Still, we are all aware of the differences among people in terms of their attitudes to laws, commandments, rules, and regulations. Some tend to see laws as absolute. Rules are meant to be obeyed. Other people adopt a more lenient attitude. The situation determines whether they feel an obligation to follow a rule in a given case. There are all sorts of variations among human beings here, of course, and we are talking about a continuum of possible behavior rather than a rigid either/or. Reading Hebrews makes it obvious that the author leans toward strict adherence to law.

The disconcerting notes in the letter to the Hebrews would probably not have been strong enough to keep it out of the canon. After all, strong words of judgment can be found in other writings of the New Testament too. Even Jesus' own words have a parallel to the rigoristic assertions in Hebrews: "Whoever blasphemes against the Holy Spirit can never have forgiveness, but is guilty of an eternal sin" (Mark 3:29). However, not only might the teachings of Hebrews create discomfort for some in the church, but there was a question about its claims to apostolic authorship as well. As you will notice when you look at the title of the book, the identity of the author is not given. In the second century, the writer seems to have been unknown. The lack of definite apostolic authorship, added to the doubts about its content, kept the letter from being accepted unquestionably in all quarters as an authoritative, inspired work.

The earliest record we possess listing the works that were considered canonical in the early church comes from a source called the Muratorian Canon, which probably originated from the environs of Rome and is usually dated sometime before A.D. 200. In comparison to our current twenty-seven-book New Testament, it adds two more works, while it does not list five of our books: James, 1 and 2 Peter, 3 John, and Hebrews. The general outlines of our present canon, therefore, are reflected in the list, but Hebrews is not among them. It is interesting to note that, by the late second century, most of the writings of the New Testament were generally accepted at least by the section of the church that produced the Muratorian Canon.[3]

You might wonder how it was that Hebrews ended up in our Bible. In the East, particularly in Alexandria, the letter was accepted early on. In the early third century, Origen, the great Alexandrian theologian and commentator, admitted that the letter was not from Paul's hand, but maintained that it presented the apostle's teaching. The general tendency in the East, nevertheless, seems to have been to view Hebrews as a Pauline writing. In the West, Hebrews was certainly well known and used by a variety of writers. Already at the end of the first century, it is alluded to extensively in a writing called *1 Clement*. Later, Tertullian, the great Latin theologian, considered it valuable and suggested Barnabas, the associate of Paul in Acts, as the author. Only in the fourth century, though, did the letter gain final acceptance in the West. By then, the letter was attributed to Paul, so that doubts about the question of apostolic authorship were resolved.

From the example of Hebrews, we get a glimpse of how the canon was developed. It is usual to distinguish three principles by which books were evaluated. The first is apostolic authorship. That is, is the author an apostle? If not, does the author enjoy the authority of an apostle? For instance, while the Gospel of Mark was not composed by an apostle, tradition held that Mark was a disciple of Peter. His Gospel is authoritative because it contains Peter's teachings about Jesus. A second principle is content. Does the writing teach a high and good understanding of God, Christ, and salvation? Is it in harmony with what we know about Jesus and his teachings? The third principle is general usage. Is the writing well known in various sections of the church, and is it used regularly by large segments of the Christian population for worship and teaching? These three principles are interrelated, of course, and all three come into play in any given situation. Still, delineating these three criteria helps to sort out what was going on in the sifting process that put the canon in its final form.

> "But who is the one who wrote the epistle (to the Hebrews), truly God knows that." (Origen, quoted in Eusebius)

As we saw, in the second century the content of Hebrews—or at least a part of that content—was seriously questioned within some circles of the church. The fact that the book could not claim apostolic authorship, since it was anonymous, further weakened the case for inclusion. However, the writing must have been circulating widely enough in the church to make it difficult to reject it out of hand. Over time, the beauty and depth of much of its content, along with the feeling that such profound thoughts must have issued from an author like Paul, led to the tradition that indeed the book had originated with him. When the church was sufficiently comfortable accepting apostolic authorship for Hebrews, the book could be included without further reservations.

Hebrews was accepted into the canon by a rather circuitous route. The irony, which you may have noted already, is that the book was ultimately accepted on the basis of an inaccurate judgment regarding its authorship. Virtually no one today believes that the book derives from Paul. Our current view that the author of Hebrews is anonymous agrees with that of the second-century church rather than with the tradition of authorship that grew up around the book later![4] We also tend to agree, though, that the primary content of the letter is rich and enriching, giving us a powerful portrait of Jesus Christ and his work in redemption that we would not otherwise possess. This one example demonstrates how the process of selecting the canon could be complex indeed.

A similar process of canonization was at work in Judaism. By the time of Jesus, most of the writings of our Old Testament were agreed upon by the Jews. However, three books remained especially problematic. They were Esther, Ecclesiastes, and the Song of Solomon. In each case, the stumbling block had to do with the content of the work. Let's begin with Esther. On the surface, the book of Esther tells a wonderful story of faith and justice in the face of anti-Semitic persecution. The difficulty the rabbis had with the book is simply that the word "God" never appears. The element of faith remains curiously vague. To use our language, the writing appears to present chiefly a nationalistic or humanitarian theme, with little trace of spirituality in evidence on its pages.

The reasons why the other two works were questioned are easy to surmise. Ecclesiastes, with its unrelenting gloom—"vanity of vanities, all is vanity"— hardly seems like an upbuilding writing of faith. Would God allow the divine, holy word to be seasoned with such pessimism? The Song of Solomon was contested for opposite reasons. There seemed to be too much joy in the book. It seemed to take too much pleasure in the world, especially with regard to sexuality. Not only was the imagery embarrassing, but, again, there is no reference to God in the book. Whether any of these three writings should be included in God's holy book was difficult for many to imagine, much less to accept. Once again, however, in all three of these cases, the writings seem to have been too well established within Judaism to be rejected. Thus, they remained part of the developing canon.

When the Hebrew Bible was finally agreed upon is debated. Most historians place the time at about A.D. 90 in connection with discussions of the rabbis at the town of Jamnia. The closing of the canon is assumed to be associated with the rabbinic movement that attempted to solidify the legal code. Their goal was to give a foundation for the Jews in the aftermath of the war with Rome. Apparently, the rabbis settled on the final list of canonical books at about the same time. Henceforth, those writings—including Esther, Ecclesiastes, and the Song of Solomon—were seen as the writings which made up the holy book.

In summary, for both the rabbis and the leaders of the early church, it was a combination of factors that guided them as they came gradually to a consensus about which books belonged in their holy scriptures. Authorship, content, and general usage all played their part in the final decisions that were made. It is important to remember, though, that the early leaders of the church did not sit down to consider each of these factors in turn. As John Barton points out in *How the Bible Came to Be*, the process of canonization was somewhat unconscious, and what little controversy there was about given books was "at the margins, not at the centre" of the canon.[5]

As congregations in the early church used these books, these three primary criteria intermingled: (1) They used these writings because they stemmed from the apostles and their content enriched their lives. (2) They approved the content of these writings because of their authorship and general usage in the church. (3) They accepted these writings as apostolic because their content was valuable and they were attested by the wider church. And so these books have been commended to us by the early church as the canon of texts that can be a source of guidance and growth in our lives as well.

> "The central core of both Testaments was never controversial in Judaism or in Christianity."
> (John Barton)

The process of composing, collecting, and canonizing the scriptures was highly complex, and it occurred over centuries, due to the diligent work of countless authors and scribes. We owe them a large debt of gratitude. The same can be said for the innumerable, unnamed people who saw to it that the scriptures continued to be preserved and passed on through the centuries. We will look at that process in the next chapter.

Questions for Reflection

- How, if at all, has this chapter influenced your understanding of the way the Bible came into being?

- As you reflect on the complex process of composition and collection of biblical writings, what impact does it have on your picture of the Bible? What bearing does it have on your sense of the Bible's inspiration and authority?

- Given what you now know about the letter to the Hebrews, do you believe it should be in our canon of scripture? Why or why not?

Chapter 2

How the Bible Came to Us

As you can imagine from the preceding chapter, the actual writing of the biblical books occurred over a long period of time. Depending on when you assign the starting point, roughly fifteen centuries elapsed between the earliest and latest writings of the two Testaments. From that time to the present, some nineteen centuries have come and gone. Much has happened in that long span of time in order to bring us the Bible as we know it today. We will highlight two sorts of things that have made it possible for us to read these ancient scriptures in our day.

Transmitting the Biblical Writings

Until the arrival of the printing press with Johannes Gutenberg in the mid-1400s, all manuscripts had to be written out by hand. That is, in fact, what the word *manuscript* means. It derives from Latin, meaning "handwritten." You can readily appreciate what a laborious process copying a book letter by letter, word by word, and line by line must have been. The work was tedious and uncomfortable. The possibilities for error were endless. Manuscripts could be utilized for a long time, but gradually they became worn and tattered. In addition, the pages themselves could become brittle as exposure to the air affected them.

As manuscripts wore out, it became necessary to make new copies. Additional copies were needed, too, because of the growth of the church, especially following the conversion of the Roman emperor Constantine to Christianity in 312. From that time onward, Christianity expanded throughout Europe. As it spread farther and farther into the smaller towns and into the countryside, more and more copies of the scriptures were needed. As new generations came and went—and, for that matter, as the centuries came and went—the need for new copies only increased.

Initially, copies were made by single scribes. Painstaking accuracy was the goal. After all, these were God's words that were being transcribed.

Nevertheless, errors frequently found their way into copies of the manuscripts. You can imagine how long it would take and how tedious it would be to copy completely just one single manuscript. Even with the best of intentions, it was difficult for scribes to make exact copies all the time.

There is a curious footnote to this procedure that may surprise you. It has to do with the broader topic of reading in ancient times. Until approximately the seventh century of our era, people did not generally read silently. Rather, they read a word on a page by pronouncing it aloud. That may seem odd until you recall that writing did not include punctuation marks, nor were there breaks between words. A line on a page looked something like this:

SINCEMANYHAVEUNDERTAKENTOSETDOWNANORDERLY
ACCOUNTOFTHEEVENTSTHATHAVEBEENFULFILLEDA
MONGUSUSTASTHEYWEREHANDEDONTOUSBYTHOSEWHO
FROMTHEBEGINNINGWEREEYEWITNESSESANDSER
VANTSOFTHEWORDTOODECIDEDAFTERINVESTIGATINGEV
ERYTHINGCAREFULLYFROMTHEVERYFIRSTTOWRITEANOR
DERLYACCOUNTFORYOUMOSTEXCELLENTTHEOPHILUS

These are the first three verses of the Gospel of Luke. You can see how much easier it is to make sense of them when you sound the words out, if only in your mind. For people in ancient times, who were not trained in reading silently, it was both normal and necessary to pronounce the words, using their lips, so that their ears could actually hear the words as their minds processed the meaning.

One other thing can be illustrated in the passage above, namely, the difficulties in copying a manuscript accurately. I have omitted two letters from the passage. If you are curious, you can try to find them. If you aren't, you can simply take my word for it! In any case, the meticulous care required to copy a manuscript without error should be obvious.

How unusual reading silently was can be shown by a story told by Augustine about his teacher, Ambrose. Ambrose was noted for his ability to read silently, without moving his lips.[1] Only in the seventh century did a change take place in this practice. A new system gradually took hold, by which spaces were placed between the words in texts. This allowed readers to comprehend individual words, and so they were able to read quietly. Still, it was normal to pronounce the words to yourself well into the twelfth century.[2]

Normally, people did not speak loudly as they read. Rather, they would whisper the words just loudly enough to hear the sound of the word in their ear. So much was this practiced that readers could be called "mumblers."[3] The reference was to the quiet mumbling sounds they made as they scanned a page. Contrary to our assumptions that libraries should be places of silence, libraries in ancient times carried an undercurrent of sound whenever people were reading.

As we have seen, a single scribe could copy a single manuscript, either alone or by listening to another person reciting the text. Already by the third, or perhaps fourth, century, a more efficient process for copying manuscripts was in use. One person would dictate, while a number of scribes would produce new manuscripts.[4] In medieval monasteries, this procedure became standard practice. A room set apart for copying manuscripts—the Bible as well as other important literature—was called a scriptorium.

With a reader dictating the manuscript to a number of copyists, it was possible to produce manuscripts relatively quickly. More and more monasteries dotted medieval Europe, and many more churches and cathedrals sprang up in towns and cities. The use of a scriptorium for copying texts made it possible to produce the ever increasing number of copies of the scriptures that were needed. Even so, the process was tedious and time consuming, requiring long hours and careful work. It is no surprise that Gutenberg's invention of moveable type changed the entire process of producing written works dramatically.

Translating the Biblical Writings

Martin Luther began translating the New Testament into German in 1521 while in hiding at Wartburg Castle in eastern Germany. The impetus Luther gave to translating the scriptures into the languages of the people was immense. However, the belief that the scriptures should be available in a language accessible to the people goes back far beyond the era of the Reformation.

The need for a translation of the Hebrew Scriptures became apparent when a large colony of Jews grew up in the city of Alexandria in Egypt. As these people became acculturated to life in the Hellenistic world, their knowledge of Hebrew became limited. As the story goes, in the third century B.C., during the time of Ptolemy II, and at his request, a group of seventy-two Jewish scholars translated the entire Hebrew Bible into Greek in a period of seventy-two days. An alternate version of the story indicates that it was seventy scholars who produced the translation, and they accomplished the task in seventy days. There is general agreement that this wonderful story is told for its inspirational value rather than for its historical accuracy. Most scholars assume that the translation was made gradually, over a period of a hundred years or more. The name for this translation, the Septuagint, comes from Latin and means "seventy."

The Septuagint has had tremendous influence on later history. As you probably know, the New Testament writings were composed in Greek. When quoting the Old Testament, the authors of the New Testament often quoted loosely, but usually they were following the Greek, rather than the Hebrew, version of the Jewish Scriptures. In addition, as the Christian gospel spread throughout the Roman Empire, the church soon came to embrace people of many ethnic backgrounds. At the same time, the percentage of Jewish adherents to Christianity gradually dwindled to a small minority. Thus, fewer and fewer people in the church could understand the Old Testament in Hebrew.

Until approximately A.D. 200, the language most frequently used in the Roman Empire was not Latin but Greek. During Hellenistic times, following Alexander the Great's widespread conquests in the fourth century B.C., the Greek language had taken such hold for commercial purposes and for general communication that it remained dominant long after the Mediterranean world passed into Roman hands. Throughout that period, a basic knowledge of the Greek language would enable you to get around in most parts of the empire.

"Ignorance of the Scriptures is ignorance of Christ." (St. Jerome)

In the early days of the church, it was only natural that the Septuagint was used along with the Greek New Testament in most of the Christian congregations scattered around the empire. Finally, in the third century of our era, Latin eclipsed Greek as the lingua franca of the Roman Empire. Not surprisingly, it was not long before the Bible in Greek became a foreign book too. The need for a translation into Latin quickly became evident.

It is worth noting that translation of the New Testament into other languages seems to have occurred early on in Christian history. Some parts of the Bible, at least, were translated into a number of other languages, including Syriac and Coptic. Parts of the New Testament were translated into Latin at an early date as well. However, the Latin translation that takes pride of place is the Vulgate. The name derives from the term meaning "common," for Latin had become the commonly spoken language in the empire.

The Vulgate is associated with the scholar Jerome, who was residing at Bethlehem in the late fourth century when he worked on a translation of the Old Testament into Latin from Greek. He had already worked on parts of the New Testament, probably revising existing Latin translations. While Jerome is not the translator of the entire Vulgate, his name is forever associated with that achievement.

The Latin Vulgate became the standard version of the Bible. It was used in the Church for centuries. After about A.D. 900, however, most people could no longer understand Latin. In the aftermath of the collapse of the Roman Empire in the fifth century, Europe gradually disintegrated into a host of ethnic, tribal groups of peoples. These peoples spoke their own languages, and Latin was foreign to them.

The result was that Latin took on an esoteric quality. It became a kind of holy language—used in the church and liturgy but unknown to common folk. By long experience, people might have a sense for what was going on in the liturgical rites of the church, but the language had taken on an aura of mystery, and there was a sense that this language had sacred power. The very words seemed to be divine.

In the later Middle Ages, some scholars began to urge that the scriptures should be translated into current languages so that people could understand what they were hearing. The hierarchy of the church resisted such attempts on the grounds that the laity would be led astray if they could read the scriptures on their own. They needed to be guided at all times by the authoritative interpretation of the church. Otherwise, they might interpret scripture incorrectly and fall into false doctrine. We will return to this argument in more detail in chapter 5.

You have most likely heard the names of William Tyndale and John Wycliffe. Both had a hand in translating the Bible into English. Wycliffe produced such a translation in the fourteenth-century. His work created a furor, but no serious repercussions came of it. Tyndale was not so lucky. Working after the Reformation had begun, he was denounced fiercely for his translation activities. He was able to live in Europe for twelve years in relative safety, but in 1536, he was betrayed to the authorities, tried, and burned at the stake.

Another aspect of the attempts to provide translations of the Bible in the common European languages is worthy of mention. John Wycliffe had been content to translate from Latin. By the time the Reformation got under way, translators were insisting on going back past the Latin to the original Hebrew and Greek texts. The Latin, they argued, is not always accurate and should not be taken as the authoritative text. This, of course, created further antagonism with the church hierarchy, which held the Vulgate in such high esteem.

Wycliffe, Tyndale, Luther, Calvin, and a host of others supported translation into modern languages out of the conviction that the laity ought to have the Bible in their own hands. Ironically, one of the arguments used by the church against translations into common languages was that such translations would lead to multiple splits and divisions in what was intended to be "one, holy, catholic" church. The history of Protestantism, unfortunately, shows how true that prediction was.

Continuing Translations in English

In the English-speaking world, there have been numerous translations of the scriptures. The most famous is the version authorized by King James I of England, which appeared in 1611. Called the "Authorized Version" or the "King James Version," it has become a standard to which all other translations are compared. It is well loved even in our own time some four hundred years later. Some groups within Protestantism continue to use it as their translation of choice. Often they claim that it is the only really reliable translation. It should be noted, however, that there was some controversy surrounding it when it first appeared. Not everyone liked it or thought that it was a completely accurate translation, and some were simply distressed because it was new and different.

Late in the nineteenth century, the sense grew that the King James Version, revered as it was, had become dated, especially because of the major advances that had taken place in the understanding of the Greek text of the New Testament. A large committee produced a new translation, the English Revised Version (RV), in the 1880s. With minor adjustments, that translation was published in the United States as the American Standard Version (ASV) in 1901.

It is almost as though these translations opened the floodgates. The twentieth century, especially the second half of it, witnessed the appearance of a host of translations. Mostly they have been produced by teams of scholars assembled for their academic or literary skills. Some translations, however, have been produced by individuals, who have sought to provide a fresh version. One such individual was J. B. Phillips, an Englishman, who began translating in wartime Britain. He published *The New Testament in Modern English* in 1958. His highly respected paraphrase is still in use. Much more widespread in the United States is *The Living Bible* by Kenneth Taylor. It has been highly popular in some evangelical circles, but serious criticisms of its accuracy and tendency to introduce theological viewpoints into the translation have led to a thoroughgoing revision of the work. Recently, a well-known preacher and teacher, Eugene Peterson, has produced a New Testament in contemporary language entitled *The Message*.

Important translations provided by committees of scholars include such works as the Revised Standard Version (RSV), issued as a complete translation in 1952. Updated in 1989 as the New Revised Standard Version (NRSV), this translation was undertaken by the National Council of the Churches of Christ in the USA. The NRSV involves a major advance in ecumenical relations, in that a version of it was produced for, and approved by, the Roman Catholic Church in 1993.

Other significant translations include the New American Bible (NAB), a Roman Catholic edition produced between 1952 and 1970, and the Jerusalem Bible (JB), likewise emanating from Catholic circles in 1966 and since revised as the New Jerusalem Bible (NJB). There is also the New English Bible (NEB), produced in England in 1970 and revised as the Revised English Bible (REB) in 1989. Along with that is the New International Version (NIV), published in 1978, and the Good News Bible, known officially as Today's English Version (TEV), which appeared in 1976.

New or revised translations in English have continued to appear at a rapid rate. You may wonder why so many different translations of the scriptures are necessary. As you will know if you have ever studied a foreign language, the work of translation is not a simple task. There are different theories regarding the best manner in which to render a thought from one language into another. In brief, three primary approaches are taken to translation. They are usually called literal, paraphrase, and dynamic equivalence.

Most translations adopt the literal approach. Here the intention is to translate word for word whenever possible. The translation will attempt to make adjustments for sentence order and other stylistic elements in the two languages. The Latin Vulgate, the King James Version, the Revised and New Revised Standard Versions, and the New American Bible are primary examples of this approach. The advantage of this approach is that the translations stay close to the original text. There is less interpretation of the intention of the writers, and so literal translations tend to represent more objectively what is in the text.

A primary problem with this approach, however, is that translations can sometimes be stilted. The correspondence between words and sentence structure between two languages is never precise. Take, for example, a single phrase in Matthew 13:19, where Jesus is explaining part of the parable of the sower: In essence, he says, "the wicked one comes." Now compare the King James Version, which reads, "then cometh the wicked one." You will notice the "cometh" almost instantly, and your first thought is likely to be that we no longer use that form of speech. Along with "thee" and "thou," this manner of speaking is no longer normal in the English language. If it does not seem odd to you, it is only because of long familiarity with the language of the King James Version itself.

Do you notice something else about this sentence in the King James Version as well? It is the placement of this same word. In contemporary English we do not normally place the verb in this location in a sentence. We usually place the subject of the sentence prior to the verb. If you are wondering why the word order in the King James Version is reversed, the answer is straightforward. The King James is simply translating word by word, and it follows the word order of the original Greek sentence. Once again, those of us who are familiar with the King James Version hardly notice this reversal.

While this translation can certainly be understood by modern readers, it would be judged to be poor English by anyone who was not aware that it came from the Bible. Literal translations run the danger of sometimes being so literal that they lose a certain stylistic beauty and quality of expression.

On the opposite end of the scale are paraphrases, which seek to make the meaning of the text as contemporary and comfortable as possible. J. B. Phillips and Kenneth Taylor both began their work with this goal in mind, as did Eugene Peterson. The advantages of a paraphrase include the fact that it is rendered in easily understandable English. To the casual reader, the Bible does not appear quite so foreign and inaccessible. The problems with such translations are that they sometimes lose, or perhaps to some degree twist, the meaning of given passages in their attempt to render them into comfortable language.

> "God, who at sundry times and in divers manners spake in time past unto the fathers by the prophets, hath in these last days spoke unto us by his Son."
> (Hebrews 1:1-2)

In the last century, the theoretical study of language and translation has become a major enterprise. Great strides have been made in understanding how language works. The implications of this for translation are enormous. The final approach to interpretation, dynamic equivalence, arises from the conviction that we will understand another language better if we translate not word by word, but thought by thought. Translators using this method search for a phrase that will render accurately the meaning and the feeling in the phrase to be translated. The New International Version is the primary translation that has adopted this approach. Today's English Version is an additional example.

The value in dynamic equivalence is that you read a basically accurate translation, yet one that flows nicely and is easy to read. The danger is that the phrases may or may not be translated precisely. After all, in the case of Old and New Testaments, translators are attempting to understand the feelings experienced by writers and readers who lived two millennia or more ago.

To see how each of these approaches works in practice, compare the following translations of James 2:16:

New Revised Standard Version: "Go in peace."
New International Version: "Go, I wish you well."
The Living Bible: "Well, goodbye and God bless you."

Notice the contrast between the literalness of the New Revised Standard Version and the paraphrase in Today's English Version. The translation in the New International Version falls somewhere in the middle between the other two.

Each version, as noted above, has its strengths and weaknesses. Which version is best depends to some degree on the setting in which you wish to use it. For example, if you are involved in Bible study, either individually or with a group, and you want to pay careful attention to the meaning of the passage you are reading, a literal version is usually best. When your goal is to read devotionally, a paraphrase can be especially beneficial. Versions adhering to dynamic equivalence are usually most serviceable when you seek to read or study the Bible in order to appreciate its overall sense, with less concern for the precise meaning of the text.

The Need for Continuing Translation

You may have asked yourself why new translations continue to be produced so frequently. Most everyone agrees, for instance, that the King James Version, as a piece of English literature, has not been equaled—much less surpassed—by later translations. Would it not be better to stay with only one translation? In one sense, the answer appears to be "Yes." If nothing else, the multitude of translations in use these days can make for some awkward moments in group Bible studies. When one person is reading from a literal translation and another from a paraphrase, the different meanings can be quite noticeable. At times, it may seem to the one person that the other is reading from an entirely different passage. The opposite side of this, as you may have experienced, is that comparing two or more versions can bring out some surprising and illuminating insights. You might well not discover them if you use only one version.

To offer enlightening insights isn't the real reason for continuing to translate the Bible, however. There are really three noteworthy reasons for new efforts at translation. One is that from time to time new texts of the Bible are discovered. Sometimes these are simply fragments of texts. In rare cases, an entire book may be discovered. The most famous example of such a discovery is the Dead Sea Scrolls mentioned in the first chapter. This collection of writings included an entire copy of Isaiah.

The earliest complete copies of biblical manuscripts that we possess come from the fourth and fifth centuries. In addition, literally hundreds of partial copies and fragments of the books of the New Testament have been recovered. Not all the readings agree. Changes may have crept into a given reading for a variety of reasons. Usually the changes are minor and have no significant effect on the meaning of the text as a whole. Occasionally, though, the readings in different fragments may differ in a way that affects the actual meaning of a phrase or sentence.

Take, for instance, Paul's comment in Romans 5:1: "Therefore, since we are justified by faith, we have peace with God through our Lord Jesus Christ." The Greek verb that is translated by "we have" actually appears in two different forms in the manuscripts and fragments of Romans. The only difference between them is that one of the vowels in the word appears in two alternative forms: either as a short "o" (omicron) or a long "o" (omega). The two letters were pronounced nearly alike in Hellenistic times, and it is easy to picture a scribe mishearing the word as he was copying a manuscript.

> "Therefore, since we are justified by faith, we have peace with God through our Lord Jesus Christ."
> (Romans 5:1)

Depending on which reading of the verb we use, we will translate it as "we have" or "let us have." The text is either a simple statement of fact, or it is an admonition. But which is it? Is Paul making a joyous proclamation of fact about those who have been justified ("we have peace with God"), or does he intend to advocate a certain manner of living in light of their justification ("let us have peace with God")?

We will leave it to the commentators to sort this out. For our purposes, it is enough to notice how different texts or fragments of texts can support a contrasting reading. Over the course of time, as more fragments come to light, they sometimes enable scholars to piece together a more exact edition of parts of the original texts. In consequence, it may also be possible to provide a slightly more accurate translation of the meaning intended by the original author.

To offer the best text possible, an entire field of scholarship has grown up over the last 150 years or so. It is called textual criticism. Bear in mind that the use of the word *criticism* does not imply a critique or a negative assessment of the Bible. Rather, textual critics compare and contrast the various copies available for each word, verse, and book of the Bible. It is a tedious process, but it has given us a highly reliable text. Nevertheless, new fragments continue to be uncovered, and sometimes they may shed further light on the original wording of a passage.

A second reason for new, or at least revised, translations is that scholars gradually come to a better understanding of some words and phrases in a particular text. Especially in the Old Testament, some words are used only once. Think how difficult it must be to translate a word when you have only one example of it.

Fortunately, many texts and fragments of texts continue to be discovered from biblical times. Some of them are biblical texts, as we have already mentioned, but many are from other literature of the times. Occasionally a newly discovered text will shed light on a curious word or phrase. At other times, as a scholar pores over a particular passage, he or she may discover a more suitable translation of that word or phrase. When enough such minor refinements have been found, it is time to incorporate them in a revised translation of the whole Bible.

A final reason for new translations is the fact that modern languages also change. In the last half century alone, American English has changed at a remarkable rate. As words fall out of use and others become common, contemporary readers gradually experience increased difficulty in understanding the text. Over a few decades, such changes do not make a vast difference, but over longer periods, translations will become dated. This is thus a further argument for the need for updating translations.

I hope this chapter has provided you with a better sense of the many people who have worked through the centuries to pass on the scriptures for later generations. They have carried out essential tasks in transmitting the texts and in translating them into current languages. In addition, countless others have worked at the exacting task of sifting through the texts, particularly of the New Testament, to ensure that we have the most accurate text possible in our hands. As I said at the end of the last chapter, we owe these people—from many generations, from many lands, and from many nationalities—our thanks for their diligence. It is wise for us to remember, especially since it is so hard for us to imagine, that many of these people gave their lives in their efforts.

Questions for Reflection

- Consider the textual question in Romans 5:1, perhaps by consulting some commentaries to see how the authors choose to interpret the verse. What difference do you think the alternative translations would make? Which do you prefer yourself?

- Choose three or four translations of the Bible and look up a number of verses in different books. See how the translations are similar and different. What conclusions do you draw from what you have found?

- What are the positives and negatives of having so many different translations? Do you have a preference for one style of translation? If so, why?

- What does it mean to you to realize that some people died rather than give up the book we hold in our hands so casually? Are any words really so important that we should be willing to give our lives for them?

Chapter 3

Divine Words and Human Words

*T*he Bible comes to us with strong claims about its divine nature as a holy book. In the words of 2 Timothy: "All scripture is inspired by God and is useful for teaching, for reproof, for correction, and for training in righteousness, so that everyone who belongs to God may be proficient, equipped for every good work" (3:16). From the beginning of the church, Christians have treasured this book, taking comfort in the faith that its words are not just the words of human beings, but rather of the Lord God, Creator of heaven and earth.

How are we to understand "inspiration"? If all of the Bible had come to us in the manner that Moses received the Ten Commandments, the process of inspiration would be clear. Exodus 20 begins with the announcement, "Then God spoke all these words." Following this is a list of all ten of the laws. The sense is simply that God has announced these words verbatim to Moses, who in turn communicates them to the people. Viewed in this light, the process of inspiration would be rather straightforward: God would speak to one or another writer. Then that writer would record precisely what God wanted to communicate. The words would thus be inspired in a direct, explicit fashion.

"All Scripture is inspired by God." (2 Timothy 3:16)

When you read the scriptures, however, it becomes apparent that the process is much more complicated than this. As we saw in the last two chapters, the Bible has come to us through a long and complex history. Further, it is not just the process of composing and preserving the Bible that appears very human. The very words, the language, and the thoughts of scripture suggest that this is a very human book. Thus, to do justice to the concept of inspiration, we must look not only at the divinity of the scriptures, but at the humanness as well.

The Humanness of the Words

It is one thing to say that the Bible bears the marks of being written by humans. It is another to look closely at the texts, focusing on just how human the words truly are. A few examples will make that clear.

Joshua 6 recounts how the people of Israel marched around the city of Jericho, trusting in God rather than in superior armaments to conquer the city. The tale sounds stirring and glorious. In fact, the entire book of Joshua describes how this inspired leader directs the people to marvelous victories that display the power of Israel's God. Intertwined with the glorious accounts, though, we encounter some all-too-human stories of death and destruction. At Jericho, all the inhabitants are put to the sword. And it is not just the people of Jericho. The residents of many other towns in the land of Canaan—men, women, and children—are slaughtered without mercy.

One particularly gruesome episode is recounted in the next Old Testament book, Judges. In chapter 4, we are introduced to Deborah, a female judge of Israel. She prophesies the Lord God's help in fighting against the king of Canaan, Jabin, who rules in the city of Hazor, in the north. Sisera, the commander of Jabin's army, takes the field against Israel. When his army is routed, Sisera leaves his chariot and flees on foot. He arrives at the tent of a man named Heber, whose wife, Jael, invites him in and promises to protect him. She hides him under a rug and he soon falls fast asleep.

What follows is graphic, to say the least: "But Jael wife of Heber took a tent peg, and took a hammer in her hand, and went softly to him and drove the peg into his temple, until it went down into the ground—he was lying fast asleep from weariness—and he died" (Judg. 4:21). You may want to ask yourself in what sense a story like this is "inspired." Why would the Lord God include such a chilling incident in an inspired scripture meant to be read by countless future generations?

There are other passages that seem somewhat out of place in the scriptures. For instance, take the curious statement in 1 Chronicles 26:18: "For the parbar on the west there were four at the road and two at the parbar." No one is quite sure what the word "parbar" actually means. The New Revised Standard Version makes a noble attempt at a translation by using the word "colonnade," but this does not help very much. You may wonder what relevance this statement has in scripture. In any case, one thing is virtually certain: you will not hear many sermons on this passage!

This verse may leave a quizzical look on our faces, but it is not upsetting. Other passages, in contrast, may be quite unsettling. What are we to make of the inspired character of a statement like this in Ecclesiastes? "For the fate of humans and the fate of animals is the same; as one dies, so dies the other. They all have the same breath, and humans have no advantage over the animals; for all is vanity. All go to one place; all are from the dust, and all turn to dust again" (Eccl. 3:19–20). An unrelenting pessimism runs through the entire book of Ecclesiastes. It seems odd that the Bible, a book of and for faith, would feature a writing with such manifest despair and desperation. As we saw in the first chapter, the pessimism in this book is so strong that it hindered its acceptance into the canon.

When you think of inspired or inspiring passages of the Old Testament, you may think instantly of the Psalms: "The LORD is my shepherd, I shall not want" (23:1); "O LORD, our Sovereign, how majestic is your name in all the earth!" (8:1); "The heavens are telling the glory of God; and the firmament proclaims his handiwork" (19:1); "Bless the LORD, O my soul, and all that is within me, bless his holy name" (103:1). These sorts of words, spoken or sung by the psalmists, do indeed draw us upward toward God. They may move our souls and thrill us with a hint of divinity. Yet there are also other kinds of words in the Psalms too. Listen to this appeal to the Lord in Psalm 58: "The wicked go astray from the womb; they err from their birth. . . . O God, break the teeth in their mouths; tear out the fangs of the young lions, O LORD! . . . The righteous will rejoice when they see vengeance done; they will bathe their feet in the blood of the wicked" (58:3, 6, 10). Even more stunning is the frustration expressed in Psalm 137: "O daughter Babylon, you devastator! Happy shall they be who pay you back what you have done to us! Happy shall they be who take your little ones and dash them against the rock!" (137:8–9). These are unquestionably human words, very human words, spoken out of suffering and loss and a desire for revenge. They may leave us wondering, though, what it means to assert, as 2 Timothy does, that "*all* scripture is inspired by God."

> "Oh, how I love your law! It is my meditation all day long." (Psalm 119:97)

All of these examples have come from the Old Testament. It is tempting to assume that the picture changes radically in the New Testament. Just think of the Beatitudes: "Blessed are the poor in spirit, for theirs is the kingdom of heaven. Blessed are those who mourn, for they will be comforted" (Matt. 5:3–4). Or recall the lovely confession, "And the Word became flesh and lived among us, and we have seen his glory, the glory as of a father's only son, full of grace and truth" (John 1:14).

We say often that Jesus Christ came to preach grace and love, compassion and peace, forgiveness and hope. Many sayings in the Gospels support that. However, Jesus also said things like, "Woe to you, scribes and Pharisees, hypocrites! For you are like whitewashed tombs, which on the outside look beautiful, but inside they are full of the bones of the dead and of all kinds of filth" (Matt. 23:27). If you read straight through one of the Gospels, you will notice that words of judgment are not at all uncommon on the lips of Jesus.

Another striking—and troubling—comment is made in Paul's letter to Titus, who was working in the church in Crete: "Cretans are always liars, vicious brutes, lazy gluttons" (Titus 1:12). You may want to make some allowance here for the hyperbole that was common in oratorical language in ancient times. You may wish to moderate the comment itself somewhat when you recognize that it is clearly intended as a generalization and is based on a common proverb. Further, you may think that the force of the comment is lessened somewhat by the fact that the proverb seems to have been a popular one. It seems to have originated some six centuries earlier with a man named Epimenides, himself a native of Crete. Still, even with all these qualifications, the charge against the Cretans has a very human ring to it. It surely leaves us wondering whether, or in what sense, such a remark may be thought to be "inspired."

The Meaning of Inspiration

The words in the Bible are truly very human words. What does it mean, then, to call the Bible the inspired Word of God? To start with, the word *inspiration* comes from a Latin root. It means "to breathe into." Interestingly, the word in 2 Timothy 3:16 that is translated as "inspired" means literally "God-breathed." The sense is that, "All scripture has been *breathed out* by God." If anything, translating it this way brings out even more powerfully the sense that God is the author of the words in this book. You may hear echoes of the creation in Genesis 1, where we read, "Then God *said*, 'Let there be light'; and there was light" (Gen. 1:3). What God's mouth breathes out is firm and certain and effective, as are the words of scripture. That is why 2 Timothy does not say only, "All scripture is inspired by God," but rather goes on immediately to talk about the consequences of God's inspiration: "and [it] is useful for teaching, for reproof, for correction, and for training in righteousness, so that everyone who belongs to God may be proficient, equipped for every good work" (3:16).

If we say that the scriptures are breathed out, or inspired, how are we to define this precisely? We can put it another way: In what manner did the Spirit of God move in the writers so that the end result of their labors was the inspired Word of God? You can imagine that this question is complex and, therefore, not easy to answer. Fierce debates have erupted regarding the mode of inspiration. This is not surprising, since our security of faith is tied to the assurance that God has given us a truly trustworthy source of revelation on which to base our faith.

The debates over the exact nature of inspiration have been much more heated in Protestant circles than in the Roman Catholic and Eastern Orthodox traditions, for predictable reasons. Both the Catholic and Orthodox traditions place much more emphasis on the institutional church as the carrier of certainty regarding faith. It is the unbroken line of succession of bishops that assures that the truth proclaimed by the apostles about Jesus Christ has been preserved continually across the centuries. Within the Protestant traditions, supreme weight has been put on the Bible as our source of faith and as the source of authority for how we live the Christian life.

The watchword for this emphasis in the Reformation was *sola scriptura,* or "scripture alone." It is one of four slogans that capture the essence of the Reformation's understanding of God's salvation in Jesus Christ. The other three are "grace alone" (*sola gratia*), "faith alone" (*sola fide*), and "God's glory alone" (*sola Dei gloria*). We will consider this rallying cry, "scripture alone," in greater depth in chapter 5, when we focus on the sufficiency of the Bible. Here I want only to note that, with this supreme emphasis on the scriptures, the question of how we should define inspiration can easily become a matter of intense debate.

> "No prophecy ever came by human will, but men and women moved by the Holy Spirit spoke from God." (2 Peter 1:21)

In fact, a host of theories has arisen in the history of the church regarding the process by which inspiration occurred. I will summarize some of the most popular. First, there are theories that picture the Spirit of God taking over the human author to such a degree that the writer becomes essentially the viaduct for the Spirit's own words. This was a popular view in the early church. It mirrors the views best known from Philo, the Hellenistic Jewish philosopher who lived in Alexandria in the first century. He understood prophetic inspiration to involve divine possession, or *mania*. This "mantic" understanding of inspiration makes prophets simply mouthpieces of the divine, and it portrays them as prophesying in an ecstatic state.

Probably somewhat unreflectively, early Christian writers depicted the inspiration of the biblical authors in this way. To cite just one example, Justin Martyr, who directed a defense of the Christian faith to the emperor in the second century, cautioned that "when you hear the words of the prophets spoken as in a particular character, do not think of them as spoken by the inspired men themselves, but by the divine Word that moved them."[1]

A second theory, closely related to this approach, is often called the dictation theory. Here the assumption is that each author is likewise taken over by the Spirit, but not in a mantic sort of way. Rather, the supervision occurs in a quieter, more functional manner. The author serves as a kind of secretary, inscribing on paper the precise words of the Spirit. There is no need for the author to be in some sort of ecstatic state, but the author's mind and pen have indeed been taken over to such an extent by the Spirit that the person serves more as a stenographer than as a true author.

It is easy to take for granted something like a mantic or a dictation theory of inspiration so long as we picture biblical writers as prophets who are taken over by the divine Spirit and prophesy according to God's will. The impetus to conceive of inspiration in this manner lies readily at hand, given the declaration in 2 Peter 1:21 that "no prophecy ever came by human will, but men and women moved by the Holy Spirit spoke from God."

However, it requires little effort to identify other styles of composition than simple verbatim prophecy in the biblical texts. The aphorisms and advice in Proverbs, for example, reveal a very down-to-earth author. So do the texts of Kings and Chronicles, which record in detail the dates, events, and genealogies of the rulers in Israel. Luke speaks of compiling a careful and orderly account (Luke 1:3), while we can easily picture Paul pacing around a room dictating his thoughts briskly to a scribe who is writing furiously to keep up.[2]

> "The books of Scripture firmly, faithfully, and without error teach that truth which God, for the sake of our salvation, wished to see confided to the Sacred Scriptures." (*Dei Verbum*, Vatican II)

The mantic and dictation theories give inspiration a very mechanical feel. In these theories, the writers appear to be controlled almost like machines in order to accomplish the divine purpose. When viewed in the light of the undeniable element of creative human involvement in the production of the Bible, both the mantic and dictation theories are clearly inadequate. For this reason, few today would adopt this kind of view of inspiration. However strongly writers on biblical inspiration may advocate the divine authorship of the scriptures, they will almost always insist that their view is distinguishable from a dictation theory. The one thing that can be said in favor of these two theories is that their goal is commendable: they seek to affirm strongly that the ultimate author of the scriptures is God.

A third approach to the process of inspiration lies at the opposite end of the spectrum from the first approach. This theory suggests that it is the personalities of the writers that are inspired. A nineteenth-century German theologian,

Friedrich Schleiermacher, can be cited as a representative of this sort of approach, but it is a common viewpoint in one form or another.[3] The assumption is that the spirits of the writers are particularly open to the divine, and they receive inspired insights which they then pass on. Here we are dealing primarily with thoughts that impose themselves on those who become authors of scripture. According to this scenario, the words, phrases, and sentences derive purely from the writer. The language, therefore, is completely human, while the underlying thoughts have a divine quality to them. On the surface, this view is attractive, for it seems to resolve the questions about the mode of inspiration relatively easily. Nevertheless, there are problems with it too.

For one thing, distinguishing thoughts and language is not so easy after all. Normally, thoughts or words come closely tied together. We don't usually formulate ideas purely and simply in our minds. At the least, if they are very specific, they are associated with words and phrases. Another problem with this approach is that it would allow us to rather casually discount anything we do not agree with. If some of the words are not to our liking, we can wave them off as only human words. After all, these inspired personalities are not expected to be infallible. Therefore, their thoughts might be inadequately expressed in the words they have written. Having drawn that conclusion, we could easily move on to describe the intended thought in ways that are more palatable to our own preferences.

A fourth approach to inspiration offers the most exacting theory of inspiration. It claims that the entire text of the Bible is inerrant. As will become evident, this view borders on the first position mentioned. It is often accused of being simply a dictation theory in disguise. Advocates of inerrancy deny that charge, insisting that the human authors are truly active in the process of composing the scriptures. We will look closely at this position because it continues to find strong support, particularly within the evangelical stream in Protestantism.

According to the theory of inerrancy, every single word and phrase in the original texts has been given by the Spirit directly and infallibly. There can be no mistakes or errors of any kind in the scriptures. We can—indeed, we must—rely on them implicitly for anything that they assert or teach.

Charles Hodge, a theologian at Princeton Seminary in the nineteenth century and the principal luminary in the Princeton school of theology, a dominant American force in Presbyterian thought, defined inspiration as "an influence of the Holy Spirit on the minds of certain select men, which rendered them the organs of God for the infallible communication of his mind and will. They were in such a sense the organs of God, that what they said God said."[4] For Hodge, the effect of inspiration is that there can be no errors in what the biblical writers intend to say. He does distinguish carefully between what the authors themselves may have thought on a given subject and what they taught. For instance, Hodge allows that the authors, as children of their times, may have believed that the earth is at the center of the solar system, but he holds that they do not teach that view.[5] Still, in everything they teach, and in the ordinary statements they make about history and other subjects, inspiration preserves them from any error.

To others, this approach sounds very much like a dictation theory, since the human authors seem to be completely under the control of the Spirit. Advocates, however, usually respond that the Spirit allows the authors to use their own styles, words, and so forth, but preserves them from any error or inaccuracies. Hodge asserts that "the inspired penmen wrote out of the fulness of their own thoughts and feelings, and employed the language and modes of expression which to them were the most natural and appropriate."[6] Underlying this approach is a deep concern to affirm that we can trust the Bible fully. It is only thus, according to advocates of inerrancy, that we can have a firm foundation for our faith in Jesus Christ.

While the intentions of this position are praiseworthy, there are some fatal flaws in the view. In the first place, the view works better in the realm of theory than in direct application to the text. That is to say, we can imagine a certain plausibility for this view as a theory: Imagining that the Lord God is going to provide a written revelation for us, we might picture God's keeping that revelation free of any error. However, as soon as we move from the realm of theory to a consideration of the text itself, it is clear that God has chosen to take a different way in providing us with inspired scriptures.

If you wish to maintain this view of inerrancy, you are compelled to do some serious juggling of the actual texts. Take comments the scriptures make on historical matters, for example. There are a number of statements that seem to be in obvious conflict with statements made in other passages. One such passage occurs in 1 Corinthians 10. There the apostle Paul is admonishing his readers to avoid evil, and he finds some handy examples in the Old Testament accounts of the wilderness journeys of Israel: "Do not become idolaters as some of them did; as it is written, 'The people sat down to eat and drink, and they rose up to play.' We must not indulge in sexual immorality as some of them did, and twenty-three thousand fell in a single day" (1 Cor. 10:7–8).

The problem is that the reference to the twenty-three thousand Israelites who perished seems to come from a story of disobedience recorded in Numbers 25. However, there the number of those who died is put at twenty-four thousand. The direct quotation about the people eating and drinking and playing cites the story of the golden calf at Mount Sinai in Exodus 32. There, as it happens, the result of God's judgment is that "about three thousand of the people fell on that day" (Ex. 32:28).

An obvious explanation for the discrepancy in the numbers might be that when Paul reminds the Corinthians of these two episodes, he simply confuses the numbers from the two accounts. This, however, would disprove inerrancy, and so those who advocate this view of inspiration are at pains to show that there is some other explanation. We won't spend more time here assessing the various attempts at explanations. My point at this stage is simply that a plain reading of the text suggests that there is a discrepancy here that most readers would judge to be insignificant to the meaning of the passage. It is significant only because a theoretical view of inspiration requires a priori that no such discrepancies can actually occur in the text of scripture.

The attempt to preserve the inerrancy of the text sometimes leads to startling suggestions. For example, Peter's denial of Jesus is probably one of the best-known incidents in the Gospels. It appears in all four accounts, but there are variations among them. The Gospel of Mark records Jesus foretelling that Peter will deny Jesus three times before the cock crows *twice* (Mark 14:30). Matthew, Luke, and John, however, report that the threefold denial will occur before the cock crows *once* (Matt. 26:34; Luke 22:34; John 13:38).

> It is agreed on all sides that our text of the Old and New Testaments is highly reliable.

This seeming discrepancy in the Gospels led one author to attempt to defend the concept of inerrancy by postulating two parts to the denial. In each, Peter denied Jesus three times. Thus, in total, Peter denied Jesus six times that night.[7] To those who are not committed to inerrancy, this construction seems to fly in the face of the writers' actual intentions when they reported Peter's denial.

Many of us wonder why such minor details must be defended as accurate, especially when they deny the obvious meaning of the text. In addition, the accuracy of such details appears to be irrelevant to the primary message of the Bible. Advocates of this view will reply that to deny inerrancy opens the floodgates to denying the doctrinal and moral teaching of the scriptures as well. If God has not preserved the small details in the scriptures, so the argument goes, how can we trust that the major teachings are reliable?

It is precisely at this point that inerrancy seems most questionable. This theory of inspiration holds that it is the original writings—the so-called autographs—that are inspired without error. However, we do not possess the original texts. In chapter 2, we looked at the process by which the texts have been handed down from generation to generation. Now, of course, it is agreed on all sides that our text of the Old and New Testaments is highly reliable. While there are indeed places that leave us uncertain of the precise meaning or the original wording, such passages rarely influence anything significant in the message of the Bible.

Nevertheless, if inspiration entails original writings that are inerrant in order to preserve the authority of scripture and the certainty of faith in Christ, then the obvious question is: Why has God allowed us to be dependent on less than perfect copies of the originals? In daily life, God not only can, but obviously does, proclaim salvation in Christ, build the church, and create faith in people of all nations without anyone's actually using an inerrant text. What then is the point of the theory? The desire of advocates of inerrancy to assert the absolute truthfulness and reliability of God is understandable and praiseworthy, but to tie that affirmation to an insistence on inerrant—but no longer existing—originals undercuts the way God has chosen to operate in human history. Thus, all of us, including advocates of inerrancy, are in the position of affirming the authority and reliability of scripture for our lives in the present, even though the copies of the scriptures that we use are imperfect.

> "The highest proof of Scripture (is that) God in person speaks in it." (John Calvin)

A fifth approach comprises a broad middle ground that in fact embraces many contrasting positions. What joins them together is the common view that, in some way, inspiration must encompass both the real input of the human author and the entire text of the writing. At various times, this general approach has been called *verbal* or *plenary* (meaning "full") inspiration. Usually, these terms are tied to inerrancy, though, and so they may be misleading. Another term sometimes employed is *organic* inspiration, since that term implies that the Spirit inspires the writers by means of some kind of inner, living process.

> "Scripture places us before the mystery of Christ." (G. C. Berkouwer)

The basic viewpoint in this approach is that inspiration does indeed deal with the actual text of scripture, in all its parts. At the same time, the full humanity of the authors must be respected. The focus, thus, is on the presence of the Spirit leading and guiding the authors as they compose their works. The Spirit ensures that the thoughts and ideas are indeed communicated, while leaving plenty of room for the authors to function as true authors. The individual writers compose their works using their own styles, words, and thought patterns. The end result, nevertheless, is a divinely inspired book.

Within the Presbyterian tradition, the Confession of 1967 tried to present this sort of understanding of inspiration when it stressed the connection of the Bible to Jesus Christ: "The one sufficient revelation of God is Jesus Christ, the Word of God incarnate, to whom the Holy Spirit bears unique and authoritative witness through the Holy Scriptures, which are received and obeyed as the word of God written."[8] The confession then goes on to speak in more detail of the manner in which the Bible has come to us:

> The Scriptures, given under the guidance of the Holy Spirit, are nevertheless the words of men, conditioned by the language, thought forms, and literary fashions of the places and times at which they were written. They reflect views of life, history, and the cosmos which were then current. The Church, therefore, has an obligation to approach the Scriptures with literary and historical understanding. As God has spoken his word in diverse cultural situations, the church is confident that he will continue to speak through the Scriptures in a changing world and in every form of human culture.[9]

Notice how this confession strives to steer a careful course, taking into account both the divine authorship of the scriptures by the Spirit and the unmistakable humanity involved in their production.

Ultimately, the process of inspiration remains a mystery. We can speak of the text of the Bible as the inspired Word of God. This book is God-breathed, but it has come in such a way that it has enlivened and enriched the biblical writers rather than overwhelmed them. As Dutch theologian G. C. Berkouwer puts it, "The mystery of the God-breathed Scripture is not meant to place us before a theoretical problem of how Scripture could possibly and conceivably be both God's Word and man's word, and how they could be 'united.' It rather places us before the mystery of Christ."[10] The process of inspiration may be elusive, in other words, but the purpose of inspiration is not.

The Purpose of Inspiration

From this discussion, it is probably evident that defining the precise nature or mode of inspiration is difficult. *Inspiration* really intends to speak of the divine origin of the Bible. For all its human character, this is a holy writing, one that derives from the Lord God. It is not just that readers can find this book to be inspiring. Many books have that quality, and we can gain profound insights as we read them. By attributing the quality of inspiration to scripture, though, we confess that the Bible is not an ordinary writing of this kind. It is not simply a common book with a respectable pedigree that can be inspiring as we read its profound thoughts and insights. Rather, while this book is indeed very human, it possesses a divine origin that sets it apart, making it truly "the Holy Bible."

As we have seen, the interplay of the human and the divine in the Bible involves some sort of organic process, by which the Holy Spirit works through the human authors. The authors maintain their human faculties intact. We see this from the authors' individual styles, as well as their linguistic and grammatical abilities. As far as all outward appearances are concerned, the writings in this book seem to be entirely normal compositions. The emotions of the various writers are often apparent. Their personal characteristics come through to some degree, and we can often gain an indication of their varying temperaments.

> God has not left us alone in the universe, and God has not left us in silence.

Yet in and through this entire work is the special operation of the Holy Spirit. God has chosen to provide us with these particular writings to offer guidance to the church in later ages. Exactly how the Spirit has worked in and with the authors in order to provide the scriptures cannot be defined easily. Sometimes theologians use the analogy of the incarnation of Jesus Christ. In the words of the Nicene Creed, Jesus is "fully God and fully man." In the mystery of the incarnation, Jesus' humanity and divinity are intertwined and completely intact in this one human being. In a similar way, so the description goes, the full human quality of the scriptures is united with the full presence of the Spirit in the process of inspiration.

For some, this is a helpful analogy. For others, it is judged to be misleading because it may suggest too readily a second incarnation of God, this time in a holy book. In any case, the precise mode of inspiration remains beyond our description. What we can say is that God has not left us alone in the universe. Life in this world is difficult and it can be dangerous, but the Lord God has not left us in silence. Rather, God has spoken through humans. God has caused words to be written down and preserved in order to show us something of who God is, who we are, and how God intends to redeem us and to relate to us in this earthly sphere. The words of this book have been given by God as a guide and blessing for our own lives.

> "For the Spirit is necessary to understand all of Scripture as well as every part of it." (Martin Luther)

To return to the Nicene Creed for a moment, we read there that Jesus Christ came into this world "for us and for our salvation." God, we might say, has—by the power of the Spirit—inspired this particular book and made it available to the church with one goal in mind. The inspired scriptures have been given "for us and for our salvation."

Questions for Reflection

- What do you think of the various views of inspiration discussed in this chapter? Which of them is most congenial to your own thoughts about how God inspired the scriptures?

- Think of the book of Ecclesiastes and the statements in the Psalms about obtaining revenge on enemies. What impact does the obvious humanness of such words in the Bible have on you? Do you consider the humanness of the Bible a negative or a positive? How so?

- From your perspective, what is the value of having an inspired Bible?

PART II The Divine Word in Human Hearts

Chapter 4

The Witness of the Spirit

*Y*ou may have heard the question, "If a tree falls in the forest and no one hears it, does it make a sound?" For our purposes, we can restate that question in this form: "If God provides an inspired book and no one opens it, does it matter?" The point is simply this: The scriptures, as inspired and wondrous as they may be, are external to us. God's Word, to be truly effective, needs to reach into our hearts. In the first part of this study of scripture, we have been talking about the Bible simply as a book—what it is like, how we got it, and what it claims regarding its inspiration. Now we need to turn our attention to the relation of the scriptures to ourselves. To begin, we will consider the witness or testimony of the Holy Spirit to the Bible.

The Illumination of the Spirit

In chapter 3, where we considered the concept of inspiration, we emphasized that inspiration deals first of all with the *text*. The concept of inspiration indicates that the words and content have a divine quality to them that are independent of the reader. The Bible is "inspired," not just "inspiring." In this chapter, then, we turn to the other side of that distinction. God's Spirit is not only instrumental in the production of the Bible, but the Spirit also works within the reader or hearer, testifying to the truth and value of its message. Thus, while we confess that scripture is itself inspired, we need to recognize that the Bible is given with the intention of inspiring us in our lives and faith. This is the internal side of what the scriptures offer—their impact on the depths of our being.

> "We acknowledge the inward illumination of the Spirit of God to be necessary." (Westminster Confession)

Early in his *Institutes of the Christian Religion*, John Calvin writes, "The Word will not find acceptance in men's hearts before it is sealed by the inward testimony of the Spirit."[1] Later he comments that the Spirit is an "inner teacher by whose effort the promise of salvation penetrates into our minds, a promise that would otherwise only strike the air or beat upon our ears."[2] Calvin is indicating that something more is needed than the simple reading and hearing of the words on the pages of the Bible. That something more has traditionally been called the "illumination of the Spirit" or the "testimony of the Spirit."

The Second Helvetic Confession opens with a declaration regarding the benefits of scripture as the Word of God: Scripture contains "the most complete exposition of all that pertains to a saving faith, and also to the framing of a life acceptable to God."[3] Then, while affirming the value of the preaching of the Word, the confession avers that neither of these will bear fruit in human lives apart from the "inward illumination of the Spirit."[4]

> "Were not our hearts burning within us while (Jesus) was . . . opening the scriptures to us?" (Luke 24:32)

Likewise, the Westminster Confession comments that the "whole counsel of God" can be found in the scriptures. Then it adds, "Nevertheless we acknowledge the inward illumination of the Spirit of God to be necessary for the saving understanding of such things as are revealed in the Word."[5]

The scriptures, we might say, provide public testimony to Jesus Christ and to salvation through him. The Spirit goes deeper, offering an "internal testimony" aimed at reorienting our hearts and directing our lives in order that we may believe in and serve Jesus Christ. Like a field that is not tilled season after season, it is possible for the scriptures to lie fallow—unused and untouched—for years at a time. This is the danger within Protestant denominations that we hear of so often these days: The Bible frequently goes unread, even among members of denominations that stress the importance of the scriptures.

Yet even when the Bible is read, it is also possible that its words will not be heard. That is to say, we may not heed the message. Our interests may go in different directions, our own desires may conflict with following the admonitions we have heard in the Bible, or our inertia may keep us from putting into practice what we in fact recognize to be God's call for our lives and actions. In the depths of our hearts, then, we may read the scriptures and hear the words clearly but be unmoved by them. We will consider this in more detail shortly.

It is hard to find a more engaging account of the impact of the divine words on human hearts than a story near the end of the Gospel of Luke. The risen Jesus meets two disciples on the Emmaus road. This seeming stranger accompanies them, speaking about the meaning of Old Testament passages in reference to the crucifixion and resurrection of Jesus: "Then beginning with Moses and all the prophets, he interpreted to them the things about himself in all the scriptures" (24:27).

As the disciples hear these words, they are touched to the quick. Later, after Jesus has broken bread with them and departed, they express their amazement at the power his words had held for them: "Were not our hearts burning within us while he was talking to us on the road, while he was opening the scriptures to us?" (24:32). Here we have a vivid description of the impact of the illumination of the Spirit. Just as the words of Jesus carried power and conviction for those two travelers, so the inspired words of the Bible are designed to engage our hearts and enliven our spirits.

There is an intensity in this encounter that is far more than what readers normally experience in the written scriptures. Only rarely will someone undergo an experience of this depth. Now and then in the history of the church, you can read about a man or a woman who is touched by an unusually far-reaching encounter with God. The great church father, Augustine, whose life and theology have been so influential on later generations, had such an encounter, as he himself describes:

> As I was saying this and weeping in the bitter agony of my heart, suddenly I heard a voice from the nearby house chanting as if it might be a boy or a girl, . . . saying and repeating over and over again, "Pick up and read, pick up and read." At once my countenance changed, . . . so I hurried back to the place where . . . I had put down the book of the apostle [Paul] when I got up. I seized it, opened it and in silence read the first passage on which my eyes lit. . . . I neither wished nor needed to read further. At once, with the last words of this sentence, it was as if a light of relief from all anxiety flooded my heart.[6]

Augustine's encounter with the Spirit of God is paralleled by others as well. In the seventeenth century, the brilliant French philosopher and mathematician, Blaise Pascal, relates an event near midnight, when he had an experience of the divine presence that seemed like fire and lasted nearly two hours. Pascal jotted down some phrases and sentences to describe the experience. Here are a few of them:

> God of Abraham, God of Isaac, God of Jacob,
> not of the philosophers and learned.
> Certitude, Certitude, love, joy, peace.
> God of Jesus Christ. . . .
> Joy, Joy, Joy, tears of joy.[7]

These intense experiences seem most frequently to occur to people of a mystical bent. Most of us will not have an experience of the magnitude of those just described. Such encounters are rare. Still, we may rest assured that if we read the scriptures, and if we live with them and allow them to permeate our hearts, we will indeed encounter their moving power in our lives. The Spirit will bring the message alive in us, assuring us of its truth and enabling us to taste its beauty.

At times, naturally, we will be moved more deeply than at other times. Occasionally, we may feel profoundly God's presence in the words of the Bible. Still, that is not the important thing. The witness of the Spirit promises that the words of scripture will come alive in us. We will recognize their truth and we will be moved to live according to them.

Cultivating a Receptive Attitude

After more than one of his parables, Jesus made the pronouncement, "Let anyone with ears listen," or in more traditional language, "Let anyone who has ears to hear, hear" (e.g., Matt. 11:15). It is possible to listen to the words of Jesus but not really hear them. The same is true of any of the words of the scriptures. We may read the words or listen as someone reads them aloud, but they may make virtually no impression on us. Clearly, not all hearing is truly hearing. There may be a number of causes for that.

"Apply your whole self to the text; apply the whole text to yourself." (John Albrecht Bengel)

On one level, a person may simply not understand the words. Take something like a vision of the prophet Zechariah:

> And I looked up and saw four horns. I asked the angel who talked with me, "What are these?" And he answered me, "These are the horns that have scattered Judah, Israel, and Jerusalem." Then the LORD showed me four blacksmiths. And I asked, "What are they coming to do?" He answered, "These are the horns that scattered Judah, so that no head could be raised; but these have come to terrify them, to strike down the horns of the nations that lifted up their horns against the land of Judah to scatter its people." (Zech. 1:18–21)

What does this mean? With the best attempt you can muster, you will probably not be able to make much sense of this statement at first glance. Most likely, you will need to consult a commentary to get some appreciation for the meaning of this passage. Not infrequently, the books of the prophets in the

Old Testament challenge our hearing because the context and the setting, as well as the literary style, are so far removed from our own time. Just to understand the meaning of the words is challenging.

If you look through the Bible, you can locate numerous other passages that are difficult to understand, at least at first glance. Some of the imagery in the book of Revelation comes to mind, but so do certain of Jesus' own parables. You might think of the parable of the dishonest servant in Luke 16:1–9, where Jesus appears to commend a conniving manager of an estate for his shrewdness. Often the notes in study Bibles or the explanations in biblical commentaries can help you make sense out of texts that are not clear. More often than you might expect, however, the commentators are not certain either. Sometimes they have to content themselves with offering a probable—or only possible—explanation. In such instances, you may take heart in the fact that even writers in the Bible itself sometimes seem to wonder what to think of another passage. Keep in mind the reference in 2 Peter 3:16 to the writings of the apostle Paul: "There are some things in them hard to understand." We may hear some biblical passages without really being able to understand them fully.

At another level, you may find that what you are reading is difficult to accept. What is your impression when you hear the admonition, "Do not resist an evildoer. But if anyone strikes you on the right cheek, turn the other also; and if anyone wants to sue you and take your coat, give your cloak as well" (Matt. 5:39–40)? Or what about Jesus' vexing statement, "It is easier for a camel to go through the eye of a needle than for someone who is rich to enter the kingdom of God" (Matt. 19:24)? And do you wonder what to do with an utterance like this from the lips of Jesus: "Blessed are you when people hate you, and when they exclude you, revile you, and defame you on account of the Son of Man" (Luke 6:22)?

Many people have found Jesus' sayings about divorce particularly perplexing. Does Jesus really mean to say what we read in Mark 10:11: "Whoever divorces his wife and marries another commits adultery against her; and if she divorces her husband and marries another, she commits adultery"? Jesus is the source of a number of similar sayings in the Gospels.

On occasion, Jesus' words create resistance in us because they imply a reversal of our normal way of looking at things. There are times when we expect a word of grace from Jesus, only to hear the opposite. Think of the "rich young ruler," for example. He is described as desirous of doing God's will as fully as possible. He has kept all the commandments of the law since his youth. His sincerity is so great that, in Mark's version of the incident, Jesus himself is moved by love for the man (Mark 10:21). If we anticipate a soothing response from Jesus, however, we will be sorely mistaken. Instead, Jesus instructs him to sell all his possessions, give the proceeds to the poor, and then return to follow him. With a note of sadness, the Gospel writer remarks, "When he heard this, he was shocked and went away grieving, for he had many possessions" (10:22).

We do not expect to hear the following response, either, to another would-be disciple of Jesus. According to Luke 9:61–62, a man addresses Jesus with what seems like a reasonable request: "I will follow you, Lord; but let me first say farewell to those at my home." Jesus' curt reply is, "No one who puts a hand to the plow and looks back is fit for the kingdom of God." Here too we might expect a word of grace or encouragement, but what the reply conveys instead is a sense of warning or judgment.

An opposite reaction may surface in us at times, when more grace is offered than we feel is warranted in a given situation. The parable of the laborers in Matthew 20 is a well-known example. Early one morning, a landowner agrees with a group of day laborers to work in his vineyard for a denarius, the normal daily wage. Four more times that day, the landowner sends additional workers into his vineyard. By the time the last group is sent out, it is dusk. Upon their return, the landowner pays all the workers the same amount: one denarius. This seeming injustice sparks an angry reaction from the first group: "These last worked only one hour, and you have made them equal to us who have borne the burden of the day and the scorching heat!" (Matt. 20:12).

> "Be doers of the word, and not merely hearers."
> (James 1:22)

We may feel sympathy for those laborers. There is something in this kind of reckoning that does not sit quite right with our notion of justice. The landowner's rather lengthy reply does not necessarily help us either: "Friend, I am doing you no wrong; did you not agree with me for the usual daily wage? Take what belongs to you and go; I choose to give to this last the same as I give to you. Am I not allowed to do what I choose with what belongs to me? Or are you envious because I am generous?" (20:13–15). We may understand the landowner's response. He is right that he is using his own money—but, somehow, distributing it in this manner seems a little unfair.

You probably realize that this parable alludes to how God dispenses grace in connection with salvation. There is a rather obvious parallel to this theme in the story of the thief on the cross related in Luke 23:42–43. One of the two criminals crucified with Jesus seems to grasp something of Jesus' true identity. He urges him, "Jesus, remember me when you come into your kingdom." Jesus' promise to him could not be more staggering: "Truly I tell you, today you will be with me in Paradise."

While this pledge may seem marvelous, I have heard people react against it, almost in anger. Is it really fair to permit someone like this thief to inherit a place in the kingdom on an equal footing with those who have spent their entire lives attempting to do good? Presumably, this man has spent most of his life as a criminal. Should he now, while he is hanging on a cross, get access to heaven at the very last moment?

Sometimes the sayings of Jesus, as well as a variety of other statements elsewhere in the Bible, are disturbing as well as challenging. They may be difficult for us to accept. In these cases, the trouble with hearing may be primarily that we do not wish to hear.

At still another level, while we may hear the words, we may not want to follow them. The parable of the wise and the foolish man in the Sermon on the Mount tells how the wise man builds a house on rock while the foolish man builds on sand (Matt. 7:24–27). Storms batter both houses, and the result is that the latter house is destroyed while the former is left unaffected. Jesus praises the actions of the wise man: "Everyone then who hears these words of mine and acts on them will be like a wise man who built his house on rock." The foolish man, in contrast, is like the one "who hears these words of mine and does not act on them."

> "The central issue about the Bible is whether we live it." (John F. Alexander)

It is clear that "hearing" does not automatically mean "doing." In many areas of our lives, hearing that we ought to do something does not necessarily mean that we will be inclined to do it. Thus, in his letter to the Romans, Paul can write rather matter-of-factly: "For it is not the hearers of the law who are righteous in God's sight, but the doers of the law who will be justified" (Rom. 2:13). Likewise, in the letter of James, we read, "Be doers of the word, and not merely hearers who deceive themselves" (James 1:22). We may understand perfectly well what a law or command requires of us, but we may not wish to do it.

Take, for example, the injunction in Luke 6. Jesus exhorts his audience, "But I say to you that listen, Love your enemies, do good to those who hate you, bless those who curse you, pray for those who abuse you" (Luke 6:27–28). Few of us could deny that to hear these words is much easier than to do them. As you read through the Bible, you will meet many more admonitions of this sort. They call us to a higher standard than may be comfortable for us. They expect a quality of life and character that may seem to be beyond our reach.

There is a brief incident in the Gospel of Luke that highlights this connection between hearing and doing in a remarkable way. On one occasion in

Jesus' ministry, a woman in a crowd of listeners, obviously moved by his message, exclaims, "Blessed is the womb that bore you and the breasts that nursed you!" But Jesus calls back, "Blessed rather are those who hear the word of God and obey it!" (Luke 11:27–28).

At the core, true hearing involves an element of will. We have to *desire* not only to know the words of the scriptures but also to follow them. Our hearts and our wills have to be captured by Christ. Even then, it may be difficult at times to follow the words of Jesus and the scriptures that testify to him. None other than the apostle Paul, in a moment of self-assessment, exclaims to his Roman readers, "I find it to be a law that when I want to do what is good, evil lies close at hand. For I delight in the law of God in my inmost self, but I see in my members another law at war with the law of my mind" (7:21–23).

In passing, I should mention that commentators are divided on the precise intention of Paul's self-description here. Many take this statement to be a depiction of Paul's condition before he came to faith in Jesus. I believe, however, that Paul's words fit better with the struggle that he finds himself facing precisely in his Christian existence. Either way you take this particular passage, there is plenty of evidence elsewhere to suggest that the writers of the New Testament considered the Christian life to involve trials and struggles.

> "Open my eyes, so that I may behold wondrous things out of your law." (Psalm 119:18)

Why is it that some people want to follow Jesus Christ and others do not? Even more disconcerting, perhaps, is the question why we—like Paul—find ourselves sometimes wanting and sometimes not wanting to follow the words of the Lord. All of this points to a "mystery of the heart" that cannot be fully explained. There are depths in our being that are not easy to fathom; there are dark corners in our hearts and wills that remain beyond the reach of rational explanation.

That we truly hear the words of the Bible, therefore, is not something that happens automatically. To hear adequately and well, our attitude is of prime importance. We need to cultivate a receptive frame of mind. How can we do that? Three words come to mind that describe the kind of attitude that is necessary for true hearing.

First of all, if we are to hear well, *humility* will be required. This most basic ingredient of our entire life with God is inculcated in various ways throughout the Bible. The significance of humility is summarized nicely in a passage in the book of James, which seems to be a loose quotation from the Old Testament: "God opposes the proud, but gives grace to the humble" (James 4:6).[8] In the following verses, amid more admonishments to submit to God, comes the lovely aphorism: "Draw near to God, and he will draw near to you" (4:8).

Along with humility, *reverence* is required. It is a question of coming to scripture with a sense for the goodness and blessedness of its teachings. As the psalmist puts it, "The law of the LORD is perfect, reviving the soul; the decrees of the LORD are sure, making wise the simple; the precepts of the LORD are right, rejoicing the heart; the commandment of the LORD is clear, enlightening the eyes" (Ps. 19:7–8). In the introduction, I spoke about the holiness of the Bible. When we approach the text with the awareness that the words on these pages are holy, we will be in a position to hear and to understand them.

Along with humility and reverence is *expectation*. You can observe this outlook readily in Psalm 119. Comprising 176 verses, this long psalm is essentially a tribute to the goodness of God's law and commandments. Notice the delight in the psalmist as he proclaims, "Oh, how I love your law! It is my meditation all day long. . . . How sweet are your words to my taste, sweeter than honey to my mouth! . . . Your word is a lamp to my feet and a light to my path" (Ps. 119:97, 103, 105).

To come to scripture with the anticipation that God will speak to you in its words is somewhat parallel to a discussion in John's Gospel, where Jesus questions whether the disciples, like the crowds, will abandon him. Peter's response is direct and to the point: "Lord, to whom can we go? You have the words of eternal life" (John 6:68).

To cultivate a receptive attitude is to adopt an attitude of prayer. In the final analysis, humility, reverence, and expectation are all essential ingredients in prayer. The appropriate attitude for prayer and for reading the scrip-

> "Only God himself is a sufficient witness to himself."
> (G. C. Berkouwer)

tures can be summarized by another verse in Psalm 119. Perhaps these often-quoted words can be our motto: "Open my eyes, so that I may behold wondrous things out of your law" (Ps. 119:18).

The Core of the Spirit's Testimony

How do we know that the Bible is true? Is there any way to be certain that the message of the scriptures is reliable? How can we be sure that we can stake our very existences—in life and in death—on the words in this book, trusting that they are truly God's words? We will look at these questions from a slightly different perspective in the conclusion, when we consider the trustworthiness of the Bible. Here I want to highlight the connection of the truth and reliability of the Bible to the testimony of the Holy Spirit.

It will be easiest to get at this topic by returning to the Reformation, where this doctrine of the internal witness of the Spirit was so highly prized.

According to ecclesiastical teaching at the time, it is the church itself that guarantees the Bible. The testimony of the church is what assures us that scripture is true and reliable. In contrast to this, Martin Luther asserted that the Bible is self-authenticating. It needs no one and nothing else to confirm its truth for us. The Bible itself, as the Spirit moves inwardly in our hearts, testifies to its own reliability and authority. As Luther explains it, "We should, therefore, not believe the gospel because the church has approved it, but rather because we feel that it is the word of God. . . . Everyone may be certain of the gospel when he has the testimony of the Holy Spirit in his own person that this is the gospel."[9]

This is not to say that the church has no role to play in our acceptance of the scriptures. It is through the church that most people learn of the faith and are directed to the Bible. Perhaps a person has grown up in a Christian family or perhaps has heard the gospel message in some sort of evangelistic or preaching setting. In whatever way, it is members of the body of Christ that have drawn a person to Jesus Christ. Therefore, it is due to the church that people are joined to the kingdom of God.

> The Spirit will not speak independently of the Bible.

Only rarely do we hear stories of someone sitting alone—in a hotel room, for instance—and encountering Jesus Christ as they read from a Bible. Even there, however, the church has had a role, because members of the church have placed the Bible where it could later be read. In fact, as we saw earlier, it is the church that has preserved and passed on the Bible in the first place. Thus, the testimony of the church does indeed play an essential part in witnessing to the value of scripture.

The Reformers did not wish to deny this role to the church; however, they did want to reject any notion that the church was the final authority, the ultimate guarantor, of the Bible's reliability and truthfulness. Referring to John Calvin's understanding of the testimony of the Spirit, G. C. Berkouwer comments that the testimony of the church can never be the ultimate ground of faith in scripture, for "only God himself is a sufficient witness to himself. The Word of God finds no acceptance until it is sealed by the inward witness of the Spirit."[10]

You can find the same line of thought in the Westminster Confession, which says on the one hand, "We may be moved and induced by the testimony of the Church to a high and reverent esteem for the Holy Scripture." Yet, on the other hand, the Confession declares that "our full persuasion and assurance of the infallible truth and divine authority . . . is from the inward work of the Holy Spirit, bearing witness by and with the Word in our hearts."[11]

Notice the last part of what I have quoted here. The Spirit is tied very tightly to the Word. The Holy Spirit testifies in our hearts *by* the Word and *in* the Word. This connection between Word and Spirit was absolutely essential for all of the Reformers. The Word in scripture cannot truly penetrate our hearts without the action of the Spirit, while at the same time we must say that the Spirit never acts in our hearts apart from the Word. Both sides of this equation are equally important.

To begin with the second half, the Reformers wished to stress that the Spirit never acts in a vacuum, so to speak. God's revelation about Jesus Christ has found its sufficient and final form in the scriptures. There will never be any new revelations, for everything is already contained in the fullness of the revelation in Jesus Christ. Thus, the Spirit will not speak independently of the Bible.

You can probably see the connection of this to our discussion of the canon previously. In particular, we confess that the canon is closed. That is, there are no more books and there is no more material to be added to it. The internal witness of the Holy Spirit works in the context of that canon. It will always be the testimony to Jesus Christ in words from that canon that the Spirit will use to awaken our hearts to faith.

Now we can return to the first half of the statement above. The Spirit's illumination is a prerequisite for us to come to trust scripture and to have its words sealed in our hearts. Here the Reformers were concerned to guard against another potential misunderstanding. Sometimes people attempt to prove that scripture is God's divine Word. You can find books that will argue for the historical accuracy of the Bible, the evidence for the resurrection, the remarkable moral teachings contained in it, and so forth. Such arguments impressed the writers of the Reformation era too. To quote from the Westminster Confession again, "the heavenliness of the matter, the efficacy of the doctrine, the majesty of the style, . . . the many other incomparable excellencies . . . are [all] arguments whereby it doth abundantly evidence itself to be the Word of God."[12]

There is clearly a place for rational arguments on behalf of the credibility of the Bible. These days, though, you can easily find other works that will argue the opposite case. They will claim, for example, that the history is inaccurate, while the moral standards are far from exemplary. Who is right? Obviously, there must be cogent reasons that point to the truthfulness of the Bible. Otherwise, we should probably throw the book away. Will proofs be finally convincing, however? Probably not. That is why the Westminster Confession, in the quotation above, says that "our *full* persuasion and assurance" arise from the inward testimony of the Spirit.

We may be drawn to the Bible, and we may find that we are uplifted by its beauty and majesty. If so, however, our love of scripture will be due not so much to a discussion of its truth claims and an analysis of whether it is a reliable document. It will be due rather to the fact that we have been enthralled by the power of its message. We have come to delight in the One of whom it speaks. And how has that come about? Solely because we have been persuaded by the inward, quiet prompting of the Holy Spirit.

> "My conscience is captive to the Word of God."
> (Martin Luther)

The testimony of the Spirit to the scriptures is, in the final analysis, identical to the Spirit's testimony to Jesus Christ. In witnessing to the truth and reliability of the Bible, the Spirit witnesses to its content. That content is the message of Christ, and it can be known—really known—only through direct experience. Thus, the appropriate way to convince people of the truth of this book is to adopt an approach similar to that in the first chapter of John. There we read that Jesus, in the process of choosing disciples, calls Philip, of Bethsaida, to follow him. Philip, obviously captivated by Jesus, looks for his brother, Nathanael, and says in essence, "We have found the Messiah." Nathanael responds with unmistakable skepticism: "Can anything good come out of Nazareth?" Philip's reply is brief: "Come and see!" (John 1:43–46).

In a sense, "Come and see!" serves as an invitation to the entire Gospel of John. It urges us to read this book, considering the words of Jesus and pondering his actions. Near the end of the Gospel, then, we are told what the Gospel writer hopes we will discover in the process: "Now Jesus did many other signs in the presence of his disciples, which are not written in this book. But these are written so that you may come to believe that Jesus is the Messiah, the Son of God, and that through believing you may have life in his name" (20:30–31).

What we can discover as we read this Gospel—or, more broadly, the scriptures as a whole—is the truth about Jesus of Nazareth. Unspoken is the fact that when we "come and see," when we discover the Christ, the Holy Spirit has been illuminating our hearts. The Spirit has been enlivening these words so that they can become words of life for us.

Questions for Reflection

- Have you ever experienced a "burning heart"? If so, how would you describe the experience? What were the results of it?

- How do you feel about some of the "hard sayings" of Jesus or about some of the unexpected ones, such as the promise to the thief on the cross?

What do you do with those passages where Jesus says and expects attitudes or actions that seem to fly in the face of fairness? Or those that run counter to our wants and needs?

- What can you do to cultivate a receptive attitude in reading the scriptures?

- How do you understand the "illumination of the Spirit," and what does it mean for your faith in Christ?

Chapter 5

Sufficiency and Clarity

*T*he Reformed tradition has been especially attentive to the way the Bible functions for individuals as they seek to experience God's grace. Along with inspiration, Reformed writers have often ascribed additional qualities to the Bible. Two of them are *sufficiency* and *clarity*. In this chapter, we turn to a discussion of both of these. As we shall see, each of these qualities helps to provide assurance that we can rely on the Bible to preserve and deepen our faith in Jesus Christ. We will look at sufficiency first.

The Sufficiency of the Bible

The Westminster Confession includes the following statement: "The whole counsel of God, concerning all things necessary for his own glory, man's salvation, faith, and life, is either expressly set down in Scripture, or by good and necessary consequence may be deduced from Scripture."[1] In short, the Bible provides enough for us. It gives us everything we need to embark on—and to complete successfully—a life of faith. You may find this somewhat surprising and may even think, "Well, I wouldn't expect anything less. Isn't it self-evident that the Bible provides what we need for salvation?"

> The real issue underlying "Scripture alone" is the meaning and authority of tradition.

To understand the intention behind emphasizing the sufficiency of the Bible, it will help to recall the situation at the time of the Reformation. In defending himself at the city of Worms in 1521, Martin Luther confirmed that his "conscience was captive to the Word of God" and that he would not change his opinions unless he was "convinced by the Scriptures and plain reason."[2] Luther may also have made the declaration at Worms that is so often attributed to him: "Here I stand; I can do no other." His assertions of reliance on the Bible produced one of the cardinal Reformation principles, *sola scriptura,* or "scripture alone." This fervent phrase became the watchword by which the Reformers critiqued the medieval church into which they had been born.

According to the Reformers, the church had gradually evolved into an institution that was corrosive to true piety and a healthy faith. Through the priests and the sacraments, the church had become an incredibly powerful system that dispensed salvation to those who lived in submission to ecclesiastical dictates. The church's life did not seem to focus on fellowship and community. Rather, the church seemed to concentrate on the hierarchy and its power over the people, which was often exercised by means of fear and guilt.

Martin Luther, John Calvin, and the other Reformers jettisoned a range of teachings that they believed ran counter to scripture. Among the significant items they rejected were such things as the doctrine that the pope is the final, infallible authority in the church, the elevation of Mary to a status of mediator between humans and Jesus Christ, the veneration of the saints, the belief in indulgences, and the concept of a fearsome way station on the journey to heaven, called purgatory.

All of these doctrines, the Reformers concluded, had grown up over the course of the centuries and negated important teachings of the scriptures. Even though these teachings were proclaimed adamantly by church authorities, the Reformers believed that they could and should be discarded.

You may sense that a deeper issue underlies all of this. From the perspective of the church hierarchy, doctrines disputed by the Reformation were by no means erroneous additions to the gospel. For the Catholic Church, these teachings too had originated with the apostles. These teachings had been passed on orally

> "We desire to follow Scripture alone as rule of faith and religion." (The Geneva Confession, 1536)

from generation to generation in the church by means of holy tradition. Thus, the real issue underlying "scripture alone" is the meaning and authority of tradition. Are tradition and scripture always complementary to each other? Are they always equally authoritative?

Let us get at these questions by looking for a moment at a concept that derives from the earliest days of the church. It is called the "rule of faith," the *regula fidei*. Earlier, we saw that the canon was developed in part to guard against heresy. To put it more positively, the canon helped to ensure that Christians would maintain the faith as it had been delivered by the original apostles. The "rule of faith" functions in a similar manner. It helps to answer the question: What doctrines or teachings do we need to hold on to in order to be sure that we are believing rightly with respect to Jesus Christ and salvation?

Originally, the "rule of faith" referred primarily to the teachings embodied in the early creeds, such as the Apostles' and Nicene Creeds. Then Augustine and others broadened the concept to include additional formal teaching within the church. Eventually, the "rule of faith" came to include all that the creeds and the church asserted to be the right way to believe and to live. Whatever teachings did not appear obviously to be part of the canon itself, that is the Bible, were believed to be based in tradition. Under the guidance of the Spirit, oral teachings of the apostles had been preserved and passed on to later generations. These teachings made up the tradition of the church, and it was as infallible and authoritative as scripture itself.

You can imagine how threatening Martin Luther's views seemed to be to the authorities in the church of his day. Not only was he denying a series of doctrines that had a long and venerable place in the church—cherished assumptions about Mary, the pope, saints, indulgences, and so forth—but he was also undercutting a basic foundation of the church's authority. Luther was contradicting the belief that there is another authentic source of revelation alongside the scriptures.

> Protestantism has often-
> times fallen victim to the
> notion that people need
> nothing at all beyond their
> Bibles.

To the hierarchy of the church, Luther's views were perceived as a rebellious attack on the institutional church and, therefore, on God as well. In response, Rome issued a papal bull in 1520 that condemned Luther's writings. Luther was forced into hiding at Wartburg Castle. In the time he spent there, he began his translation of the Bible into German.

It is unfortunate, but hardly surprising, that the ecclesiastical authorities were not interested in dialogue about Luther's positions. While there was some recognition of abuses in the church, there was little sense for the depths of the theological issues that Luther had placed on the table. You can see this in the official response of the Catholic Church, which came at a council, held at Trent, in northeastern Italy. The council opened in 1545 and continued on and off through 1563. In its deliberations, the Council of Trent attempted to clean up the obvious abuses in ecclesiastical life, but it upheld the major teachings that Luther and other Reformers were questioning.

Most significant for us here is the declaration made by the Council of Trent on the relation of scripture and tradition. After stating that the gospel is "the source at once of all saving truth and rules of conduct," the council declared, "It also clearly perceives that these truths and rules are contained in the written books and in the unwritten traditions, which received by the Apostles from the mouth of Christ Himself, or from the Apostles themselves, . . . have come down to us, transmitted as it were from hand to hand."[3]

The language of Trent sounds as though it is affirming two distinct sources of revelation. Scripture and tradition are believed to be in harmony with each other, for they both derive ultimately from the apostles. Still, scripture and tradition are presented as though they are independent sources, and both are to be given equal reverence and authority.

You can imagine the import of Luther's denial that scripture and tradition stand on the same footing. To disavow the authority of tradition is to undercut much of the edifice of the medieval church, because the majority of its most significant teachings cannot be found clearly in the scriptures themselves. Rather, such doctrines developed over time as the church unfolded across the centuries. For the Catholic Church, this is sufficient, since tradition is equally authoritative with the Bible. For the Reformers and for the Protestant movement in the following centuries, though, the teachings of tradition are not necessarily correct. Tradition by itself is viewed as an insufficient foundation for truth. Only as such teachings are tested and approved by the scriptures can they be affirmed to be valid and true. Once again, we hear in the background the slogan of the Reformation: "scripture alone."

> "Scripture" and "tradition" need not be seen as opposites.

Until the middle of the twentieth century, both Protestants and Catholics were inclined to operate from defensive positions. Frequently, in discussions of each other's views, writers tended simply to castigate the other side. Often there was little effort made to see deeper, positive reasons for the opposing positions. Fortunately, much of that has changed, and—even when disagreement on specific teachings continues—there seems to be much more appreciation for the motives behind differing teachings.

The changed environment is due to a large degree to the remarkable openness and creativity that emerged at the Second Vatican Council in the 1960s. Among many other topics, the council took up the issue of whether, as the Reformation had charged, the Catholic Church embraces two separate, equally authoritative sources of revelation. Does the Catholic emphasis on tradition damage the sole authority of the Bible? In a document published in 1965, entitled the *Dogmatic Constitution on Divine Revelation (Dei Verbum)*, the council attempted to clarify the unity of scripture and tradition:

> There exist a close connection and communication between sacred tradition and sacred Scripture. For both of them, flowing from the same

divine wellspring, in a certain way merge into a unity and tend toward the same end. . . . [I]t is not from sacred Scripture alone that the Church draws her certainty about everything which has been revealed. Therefore both sacred tradition and sacred Scripture are to be accepted and venerated with the same sense of devotion and reverence. Sacred tradition and sacred Scripture form one sacred deposit of the word of God, which is committed to the Church.[4]

The Second Vatican Council definitely rejects the idea that scripture and tradition form two separate sources of revelation. Likewise, Catholic theologians have emphasized strongly that the Council of Trent should not be read to imply two independent sources of truth. Nevertheless, within Catholic theology, tradition continues to be viewed as the authoritative interpretation of scripture. To Protestant theologians, therefore, this formulation still seems to infringe on the principle that it is "scripture alone" that is authoritative. It still seems to suggest that the Bible is not really sufficient. The formulation implies that something further is needed for the Bible to operate effectively.

> "These Holy Scriptures fully contain the will of God, and whatever people ought to believe unto salvation is sufficiently taught in them." (Belgic Confession of Faith, 1619)

We should note that the Catholic tradition is correct in seeing tradition as an important element in our understanding of the Bible. There is definitely a danger if tradition is downplayed too much. If Catholicism has erred on the side of making tradition the final authority, Protestantism has oftentimes fallen victim to the notion that people need nothing at all beyond their Bibles. The individualism inherent in the Protestant tradition has led some people to believe that they are sufficient unto themselves. "Just me and my Bible" is their slogan, and it can lead to damaging misinterpretations and misunderstandings of the Bible.

For example, I have heard people say that they do not believe in commentaries; it is best, they say, just to read the Bible alone. Curiously, in my experience, those people have frequently belonged to groups that cherish the so-called Scofield Bible. This is an edition of the King James Bible that includes extensive and very detailed notes by C. I. Scofield, an early twentieth-century English clergyman. It has always seemed somewhat humorous to me that these people could be so reliant on those notes, while insisting on the need to read the Bible alone. Why the Scofield notes do not qualify as a commentary on the text, I do not know!

The more serious issue in this situation is that those who claim to follow the Bible purely and simply, without using any other sources, may well overlook the traditions that are operative in their own communities. By being unaware of their own tradition, they are more likely to be uncritical about their beliefs and ways of doing things. As a result, over time their unexamined traditions can become petrified. They may in fact become more locked into rigid traditions than are others who emphasize the importance of tradition.

It is important to bear in mind that scripture and tradition need not be seen as opposites. In themselves, they are not contradictory. Likewise, in spite of the fact that tradition often carries negative connotations in the contemporary world, it is, in fact, a good thing. The apostle Paul speaks of tradition when he refers to passing on the Christian proclamation regarding Jesus' death, burial, and resurrection: "For I handed on to you as of first importance what I in turn had received: that Christ died for our sins in accordance with the scriptures, and that he was buried, and that he was raised on the third day in accordance with the scriptures" (1 Cor. 15:3–4). The apostle continues with a listing of those who have seen the risen Lord. Here I want to focus on the words "handed on." This term, along with the words "what I received," reflects the language of the rabbis. The language relates to the process of passing on the tradition of Israel's faith from teacher to pupil.[5] To pass on the tradition faithfully was of paramount importance for the rabbis, and the same was true for Paul.

> "Jesus Christ is the one Word of God which we have to hear, trust and obey."
> (Barmen Declaration)

Marjorie Thompson has this to say about the value of tradition:

> Tradition tracks a living faith through its history, helping us find markers that let us follow the path today. Some of those markers allow us to enter into the peculiar world of scripture so that it again becomes a vital Word for us. . . . While not all of tradition is worth preserving, there are so many riches to be recovered from its storehouse that we should be glad to sift the treasures from the sand in which they are buried![6]

On the one hand, it is tradition that keeps us rooted in the wisdom of the past. On the other, it is this wisdom that can enrich our lives in the present. The difficulty, from a Reformed perspective, is only in making tradition equally authoritative with scripture. The Bible does not need something further to explain or to supplement its message. Its presentation of the message of salvation in Christ is not inadequate or imperfect. It is indeed sufficient in itself.

What does affirming the sufficiency of the Bible mean for us today? First, the sufficiency of scripture means that we do not need any additional source of information or revelation. We have already noticed how this relates to tradition as an authoritative interpretation, but we can take it in other directions. Some people suggest that additional literary writings should be included in the scriptures. We possess wonderful and profoundly moving literature in such writings as Augustine's *Confessions,* John Donne's poetry, and Mother Teresa's writings. Each of these, and many others as well, can have an inspiring effect on us. Should we not also include such inspiring writings in the Bible?

This is the point of maintaining a concept of the canon, as we saw in chapter 1. Many writings—whether from the Christian tradition or from other traditions—can provide us with inspiration and foster spiritual growth. Only some writings, however, are part of the foundation of our faith in Jesus Christ. Only those books produced in Israel and the apostolic church belong to the beginnings. Thus, works that are produced later, no matter how rich in content, do not become part of the canon. They offer instead telling testimonies to the impact of the message that is already contained in the canon.

> "In the sacred books, the Father who is in heaven meets His children with great love and speaks with them." (*Dei Verbum, Vatican II*)

The Bible is sufficient without such additional writings, however enriching and uplifting they may be. The same point applies to other groups that claim to have received further revelations in later centuries. A classic example is the Book of Mormon, which members of the Latter-day Saints claim has equal authority with the scriptures of the Old and New Testaments. Another example might be the writings of Ellen White. She is so highly revered among Seventh-day Adventists that claims are often made for the infallibility of her writings.

In these traditions, the authoritative status given to writings that have derived from leaders of the movements implies that the scriptures can be supplemented either by additional revelations or by official interpretations. In contrast, Reformation churches would affirm that no further revelations are necessary. All that we require for faith in Jesus Christ is contained in the Bible. It is sufficient for all our needs.

To see how significant this point is, we can view it from yet another angle. Recall the rise of the National Socialist movement in Germany in the 1930s. Tremendous pressure was soon applied to the church to stand firm as a loyal supporter of Nazism. Good "German Christians" were expected to support the Reich in all of its policies and practices. In May 1934, a group comprised predominantly of pastors and church members gathered at Barmen. Their search for a solid basis to resist the encroachments of the regime on the church led to a statement of faith. Authored primarily by the Swiss theologian Karl Barth, the document was entitled, "The Theological Declaration of Barmen." It became the foundation for the Confessing Church, the movement in the church that resisted Nazism.

Reading this declaration—or "Barmen," as it is often called—you can readily hear strains of Martin Luther's "Here I stand." The document challenges readers to test its claims: "If you find that we are speaking contrary to Scripture, then do not listen to us! But if you find that we are taking our stand upon Scripture, then let no fear or temptation keep you from treading with us the path of faith and obedience to the Word of God."[7]

To take a stand in this political situation was dangerous, and it must have been supremely frightening. Nevertheless, many did indeed resist the Reich's demands, claiming that "Jesus Christ, as he is attested for us in Holy Scripture, is the one Word of God which we have to hear and which we have to trust and obey in life and in death."[8] Here Barmen's declaration offers an excellent example of the Reformation claim regarding the sufficiency of scripture. "We reject," the document goes on to state, "the false doctrine, as though there were areas of our life in which we would not belong to Jesus Christ, but to other lords."[9] Thus, political movements and social doctrines, just like additional writings and further revelations, are excluded from equal standing with the scriptures. The Bible is sufficient without them. And sometimes, as we have just seen, the Bible may be sufficient in opposition to them.

Sufficiency also means for us that we have a source of comfort and support in the face of the mysteries of life. Especially in those times when tragedies and troubles enter our own lives or the lives of families and friends, we can hold fast to the scriptures. Many people have testified to experiences when the Bible's sustaining power has brought comfort and peace in long hours and dark days. Most pastors will remember times when they were called to the bedside of a man or woman who had been wasted away by disease but was still clinging to a thread of life. Simply reading from the scriptures provided reassurance as well as a sense of peace and care. Through the words of the Bible, by the power of the Spirit, the message of God's eternal love and grace in Jesus Christ has often brought consolation and serenity to a person who is suffering and is in uttermost need.

The Bible can be a source of help whenever we have to ask the hard questions of life, such as: Why do people suffer? Why do loved ones perish in accidents or wither away in slow and painful deaths? Why do family members harm one another or friends betray one another? We can talk about such concerns endlessly, but ultimately they remain unanswered questions. As we all know, there are mysteries to life that we cannot unlock.

The scriptures do deal with such questions, of course. Picture Job, cursing the day he was born (Job 3:1–5). Or remember David, grieving over the deaths of two sons and facing the irony that it is his own behavior that has led to such awful consequences (2 Sam. 12:16–23; 18:31–33). Consider Hannah, crying her eyes out because she has been childless for so many years (1 Sam. 1:7–18). And imagine Naomi, living in a foreign land and confronting the loss not only of her husband but of both her sons as well (Ruth 1:3–5).

The Bible knows about grief, and sadness, and despair. It understands that troubles come and life seems pointless. It doesn't give answers, as Paul found out when he prayed and prayed about what he called a "thorn in the flesh," appealing for it to be removed from him (2 Cor. 12:7). The Bible does not give answers, but it does provide hope. This is another thing that the Reformed tradition means by the sufficiency of the Bible. We do not get everything we want from the Bible, but we do get enough. Put differently, the Bible does not give us complete knowledge, but it does give us essential knowledge.

In the inspired scriptures, God has provided everything that we human beings need in order to make our way through this life. The pages of the Bible contain what is necessary to enable us to trust in Jesus Christ. It is in this sense that, as we seek to live with wisdom and integrity, the scriptures are sufficient for us.

The Clarity of the Bible

The Reformed tradition has ascribed another quality to the Bible—clarity. In brief, this quality indicates that the Bible is not an obscure document. Its primary meaning is plain, and it can be understood by any reader.

At first glance, you may wonder whether the Bible is really all that clear. In chapter 3, we have already noticed some passages that are so obscure that no one knows for sure what they mean. (Remember the "parbar" from 1 Chronicles 26!) Likewise, many of the prophecies from Old Testament writers may leave us shaking our heads in wonder. To whom is this written? Why is the prophet so angry? What does he mean with that analogy or metaphor? The questions that such passages raise for us may lead us to dispute the idea of the clarity of the scriptures.

> "The clarity of Scripture" means that its primary meaning is plain, and it can be understood by any reader.

On another level, you may also wonder how clear the Bible is, given that frequently there has been sharp disagreement among different denominations about basic scriptural teachings. Here I am not thinking just of differing views on minor issues. Some major teachings in our churches are understood differently, based on divergent interpretations of specific biblical passages. We will speak in more detail about interpretation in the next two chapters, but here it is important to notice how profoundly a dispute about an interpretation of a passage may undermine the claim that the scriptures are clear.

We will take two examples. First, recall Jesus' words about the bread at the Last Supper in Matthew 26:26: "Take, eat; this is my body." The words seem straightforward enough. Yet this is the fundamental point that shattered attempts to bring unity between the Lutheran and Reformed streams at the time of the Reformation. In 1529, at Marburg in Germany, Martin Luther met to discuss with Ulrich Zwingli, the Swiss Reformer from Zurich, their views of the presence of Christ in the Lord's Supper. Zwingli argued that the use of Jesus' words, "This is my body," should be taken figuratively. Luther, while agreeing that language can be used figuratively, denied that the meaning could be any other than literal here.[10]

The two viewpoints, Lutheran and Reformed, could not be reconciled, and the continuing disagreements on this issue kept the German and Swiss streams of the Reformation from any hope of unity. One side in this debate was absolutely certain that the Bible should be understood literally in this passage. The other side was equally certain that the Bible should be understood metaphorically. So, you may ask yourself, how clear are the scriptures themselves? Even the central sacrament of the Christian faith can give rise to conflicting views.

We will draw our second example from the sacrament of baptism. For those in the Baptist tradition, it is an article of faith that only "believers" should be baptized. The appropriate age to permit baptism can vary to some degree, but the Baptist tradition steadfastly rejects infant baptism. Most other Protestant denominations do baptize infants, as do the Orthodox and Roman Catholic traditions. Usually these denominations are equally adamant that infant baptism is the correct procedure to follow with children born of Christian parents.

All sides want to cite scriptural warrant for their positions regarding infant baptism. One passage that is often cited is Acts 16. This chapter relates an interesting story about Paul's and Silas's adventures in the town of Philippi. They had been imprisoned on account of their evangelizing work. About midnight an earthquake shook the town and the prison doors came open. Assuming that the prisoners had escaped, the jailer was about to take his own life when Paul called out to him, saying that they were still there. This amazing occurrence convinced the jailer that the message of Christ was true, and so he asked how he too could be saved. Paul's answer was, "Believe on the Lord Jesus, and you will be saved, you and your household" (Acts 16:31). Shortly afterward, the jailer was baptized. The precise words in the text are, "then he *and his entire family* were baptized without delay" (v. 33).

For the Lutheran and Reformed traditions, among others, this verse provides ample evidence that infant baptism is the appropriate manner to treat children within a Christian family. The entire household, the text tells us, was baptized. For Baptists, in contrast, the passage means only that all those who can make their own confession of faith should be baptized. The comment about the "entire family" is intended simply as a general statement. It does not need to be applied to every single individual in the household.

Both sides in this discussion buttress their viewpoints with a variety of other texts in the Bible, and both sides take what sometimes sounds like an almost prideful pleasure in maintaining that their own position is correct. In my view, the only certainty here is that the two sides will not come to agreement any time soon!

We could multiply such issues with ease. Just think of the disputes over such things as predestination and free will, the priesthood and apostolic succession, Sabbath observance, or the meaning of the millennium in the book of Revelation. Christians of goodwill have regularly disagreed with each other, sometimes intensely, over the proper understanding of these and many other topics. In light of all of these conflicting opinions, what does it mean to claim clarity for the scriptures? Doesn't the Bible often appear to be anything but clear? Isn't the Bible really rather hard to read, especially because it comes from a cultural and historical setting that contrasts so greatly with our own?

> "The clarity of the Bible" focuses on the basic message of the scriptures.

The Reformers were certainly aware of these kinds of difficulties in reading the scriptures. Nevertheless, from Martin Luther onward, the clarity of the Bible became a cardinal teaching in Reformation congregations. To understand the import of this affirmation, we need to consider the setting at the beginning of the Reformation era. As we noted in chapter 2, long before the time of Luther, the church had kept the laity from reading the Bible on their own. In the view of the ecclesiastical hierarchy, interpreting the scriptures was not something that could be left to laypersons, for fear that they would too readily misinterpret the text and fall into error. For the medieval church, the Bible was not a clear book. It was seen rather as a somewhat obscure book, one that was more likely to confuse and harm individual readers than to increase their faith.

With this sense that the Bible is really an obscure book, the only protection against misunderstandings and errors was to limit the scriptures to a special class, trained in proper interpretation. In practice, this meant that the Bible was reserved for the hierarchy. When people like John Wycliffe, William Tyndale, and Martin Luther wished to translate the Bible into the common languages, they were thus transgressing a basic tenet of the medieval church. When possible, the church suppressed these translations. In the case of William Tyndale's translation, which appeared in 1526, the bishop of London purchased large numbers of copies and had them burned in public.

Given the spirit of the times, it is no wonder that the translators themselves were in danger. If they were in reach of ecclesiastical authorities, they might well be executed. As noted earlier, Tyndale was burned at the stake in 1536. Approximately one hundred years earlier, John Wycliffe's body had been exhumed in order to be burned. Luther survived, but only because he lived under the protection of a favorable ruler.

In passing, we may note that the Catholic position following the Reformation continued to be one of suspicion toward vernacular translations. It was only at the Second Vatican Council that a major change in the official position of the church became evident. The *Dogmatic Constitution on Divine Revelation (Dei Verbum)* asserts, "Easy access to sacred Scripture should be provided for all the Christian faithful."[11] Further, the document encourages bishops to make arrangements for translations with suitable notes. They are also instructed to educate laypersons in proper scripture reading so that they can "safely and profitably grow familiar with the sacred Scriptures and be penetrated with their spirit."[12]

The sea change in the Catholic attitude to the Bible over the last decades is evident from the fact that Bible translation teams now regularly include both Protestant and Catholic biblical scholars. The New Revised Standard Version is a case in point. When this revision of the Revised Standard Version was being prepared, the committee included a number of Roman Catholic scholars as well as an Eastern Orthodox representative. The new translation was published in 1989. Shortly thereafter, a version with minor changes was published with Catholic readers specifically in mind, and it received official approval by the Roman Catholic Church.

> The lack of unity among believers in Jesus Christ is a sad commentary on our failure to truly live by the words of scripture.

Returning to the Reformation, we have seen that the accent on the clarity of scripture arose in a context in which Bible reading by the laity was regarded with suspicion. The Reformers stressed that the Bible should not be seen as an obscure book. Its message is understandable by all who have the opportunity to read it, from the most educated of scholars to the simplest of the faithful.

Here we need to look more closely at what the Reformers did and did not mean when they spoke about this quality of scripture. In the first place, the clarity of the Bible focuses on the basic message of the Bible. The Reformers did not mean to suggest that every word in these sixty-six books (by the Protestant reckoning) is clear and easy to understand. Within scripture itself there is an admission of how difficult some writings can be. If you have ever had trouble grasping something written by the apostle Paul, you will appreciate the comment near the end of 2 Peter. The writer, in summing up the admonitions in the letter, has this to say: "So also our beloved brother Paul wrote to you according to the wisdom given him, speaking of this as he does in all his letters. There are some things in them hard to understand, which the ignorant and unstable twist to their own destruction, as they do the other scriptures" (2 Peter 3:15–16).

Evidently, Paul's letters were already recognized as being on a level with other inspired writings, but they were also perceived to be deep and somewhat difficult. Patience and effort, therefore, are required to follow the wisdom in Paul's letters. If you have ever tried to figure out Romans 9–11, where Paul reflects on the fate of Israel, you will understand exactly what is meant here. The same can be said not only for many other passages in Paul but also for many other texts in the Bible as a whole. Much of what we call God's inspired Word is neither very clear nor very easy to understand.

In the second place, the clarity of the Bible does not mean that interpretation is not necessary. Rather than deny the need for interpretation, the Reformers established a fundamental principle regarding correct interpretation: Scripture is self-interpreting, that is, "scripture interprets scripture." What may be unclear in one place should be understood in the light of other, more obvious passages. The Westminster Confession states this principle succinctly: "The infallible rule of interpretation of Scripture, is the Scripture itself; and therefore, when there is a question about the true and full sense of any scripture . . . it may be searched and known by other places that speak more clearly."[13] This quotation is representative of the position of the Reformation. Outside authorities and extraneous sources are not determinative in the proper understanding of the Bible. When clarity about a given text is sought, the appropriate source to consult is other parts of scripture.

There is a telling story in Acts 17, which may help to illuminate the clarity of the scriptures. Paul and his partner, Silas, arrive in the town of Beroea, in Macedonia. As they often do, they seek out the synagogue and begin preaching to the Jews there. Apparently, the people in Beroea are particularly enthusiastic about hearing and understanding this new message. The text tells us that "they welcomed the message very eagerly and examined the scriptures every day to see whether these things were so" (Acts 17:11). The scriptures they were consulting, of course, were those of the Old Testament.

The attitude of the Beroeans reflects what Luther and the other Reformers wished to affirm when they insisted on the clarity of the scriptures. Individuals, even though they lack specialized training and education, are able to read the Bible and make sense out of it. The Bible is not a closed book. It is not accessible only to a well-trained class of interpreters. Instead, it is a book that contains the words of life. Scripture is meant for, and open to, all people.

I want to insert a final note of caution here. G. C. Berkouwer once wrote that there is no more disturbing affirmation concerning the Bible than this confession of its clarity.[14] The basic message of the scriptures is clear, he wrote, yet the divergences in interpretation of the Bible among Christian denominations have often produced serious division and discord. The lack of unity among believers in Jesus Christ is a sad commentary on our failure to truly live by the words of scripture.

The intention of affirming the clarity of scripture is not to claim that everything in this book is obvious and explicit to any reader. Reading the Bible is not straightforward in the sense, say, of looking up a number in a telephone book. Clarity is present as we come to the Bible in faith. The scriptures are clear as we entrust ourselves to the Christ they speak about and as we rely on the power of the Spirit to illumine our minds and hearts. To quote Berkouwer once again, the clarity of scripture is "a promise and a task."[15] The promise is this: As we read in faith, scripture will be clear to us. The task: We must seek the clarity of the Bible by coming to it with humility and faith.

Questions for Reflection

- What is your response when you hear the word *tradition*? In what ways might tradition be helpful? When might it be questionable? What place do you think tradition should have in the church?

- What does it mean to say that scripture is *sufficient*? What does the sufficiency of the Bible mean for you?

- What does it mean to say that scripture is *clear*? What does the clarity of the Bible mean for you?

Chapter 6

Do You Understand What
You Are Reading?

Some years ago, I was attending a chapel service in the college where I was teaching at the time. A minister from a local congregation had been invited to deliver the sermon. He took as his theme Revelation 21. About midway through a meditation on the end times, he paused to point us to verse 2: "And I saw the holy city, the new Jerusalem, coming down out of heaven from God, prepared as a bride adorned for her husband." I perked up my ears when he explained that this verse gives us the clue regarding the location of God's final kingdom. When this old, tired earth gives way to a new, eternal world, he asserted, we will live in the sky. The reason? Revelation mentions the new Jerusalem descending, but it never says that it arrives on the earth. Thus, the final residence for God's people will be in a place suspended between heaven and earth.

> "Do you understand what you are reading?"
> (Acts 8:30)

The Need for Interpretation

While this preacher was undoubtedly serious about the scriptures, he failed to notice the highly figurative language in the book of Revelation. Even the verse he had quoted about the new Jerusalem contains a figure of speech. It compares the new city to a "bride adorned for her husband." Middle Eastern weddings normally included a procession in which the adorned bride was brought to her husband-to-be. In some of the villages of Palestine, this is still practiced. The fact that the writer does not mention the actual arrival of the bride (that is, the new Jerusalem) does not suggest that she never arrived at the place where the marriage ceremony was to be celebrated.

The misunderstanding of the passage arose because the minister was trying to derive literal information from a highly figurative passage. This is not really so surprising; our human curiosity often tempts us to desire more infor-

78

mation than is available. In many more areas than Bible study it seems to be the case that the more information we can assemble, the more secure we feel. This preacher wanted information about the end times. The problem was not that he was interpreting the text. The difficulty was rather his apparent inability to interpret the text adequately. Interpretation is certainly necessary if we are to understand the Bible properly. That is clear from scripture itself.

In the early days of the church, the book of Acts records a story about Philip, one of the apostles. He is sent by an angel to a desert road on the route from Jerusalem to Gaza (8:26). There he meets an official in the government of the queen of the Ethiopians who is returning from Jerusalem. The official is a eunuch. Eunuchs were employed as guardians and servants, especially on behalf of the women of the ruling class. Often these men became trusted servants, and they sometimes moved into important governmental positions. Since this eunuch had been worshiping in Jerusalem, he was clearly practicing in some fashion the Jewish faith. Probably he was a "God-fearer," that is, a non-Jew who worshiped the God of Israel but did not take on all the laws and rituals of Jewish practice.

When Philip encounters the man, he is reading from the book of Isaiah. As we saw in chapter 2, the Ethiopian would have been reading aloud. Philip's question takes us to the heart of our present chapter: "Do you understand what you are reading?" You can detect a hint of frustration in the response: "How can I, unless someone guides me?" (8:30–31). The passage that the eunuch has been reading comes from Isaiah 53. Here the suffering servant is portrayed as one who is like a sheep "led to the slaughter" and "a lamb silent before its shearer," one who is humiliated, denied justice, and killed (8:32–33). Philip points out that this reading refers to Jesus. Then he proceeds to proclaim the gospel to the eunuch. Shortly thereafter, the eunuch catches sight of a pool of water, and he requests to be baptized. Philip obliges, and the eunuch continues on his journey home.

This story highlights a number of points about interpretation. First, and very simply, another human being, who does understand the scriptures, enables the eunuch to arrive at a sensible interpretation. We have a reminder here that God does not operate in a vacuum. Instead, the Lord works through the church to make the Bible effective in human lives. For this reason, Bible study should regularly be conducted in the context of the Christian community. While you can definitely read the Bible with profit on your own, over the long haul it is important to read the scriptures along with others. Interaction with others helps us see how best to understand the Bible in our own setting.

A second item worth noting is that, although the story does not specifically say that the Holy Spirit illuminates the eunuch's mind and heart, it is evident that the Spirit underlies the entire process by which Philip and this man meet. As we saw in chapter 4, the testimony of the Holy Spirit working within us is what ultimately makes understanding and accepting the message of Jesus Christ fruitful. This same testimony of the Spirit provides the foundation for the process of interpreting the Bible properly.

Third, Philip's explanation of the text from Isaiah offers a good example of the ultimate purpose of all texts: They point us to Jesus Christ. We will talk shortly about various levels of meaning in biblical passages, but here it is important to underscore the fact that the purpose of the whole of scripture is to draw us close to Christ. In the words of 2 Timothy, the sacred scriptures "are able to instruct you for salvation through faith in Christ Jesus" (2 Tim. 3:15). Or as the Gospel of John puts it: "These [things] are written so that you may come to believe that Jesus is the Messiah, the Son of God" (John 20:31).

Fourth, this story underlines the need for looking carefully at the text in order to understand its meaning adequately. When the eunuch asks Philip about the meaning of the quotation from Isaiah the prophet, he asks, "About whom, may I ask you, does the prophet say this, about himself or about someone else?" (Acts 8:34). Even if the quotation were related only to the prophet himself, we might wonder how literally it is meant: "Like a sheep he was led to the slaughter, . . . For his life is taken away from the earth" (8:32–33). Philip understands the words to refer beyond Isaiah's time. They entail a reference to the life of Jesus centuries later.

Literal and Figurative Interpretation

From day one in the church, one of the main difficulties in understanding biblical passages has revolved around the question of whether they are intended literally or figuratively. Figurative language itself can easily confuse us. I remember an incident from my own experience in the church in which I grew up. At each service of baptism, the minister would regularly include a lovely line in his prayer for the infants whom he had just baptized. He would invariably request that their "names be written in the lamb's book of life." As a youngster, hearing those words, I pictured the babies as young lambs and imagined that the minister was praying for their protection in this world. I was old enough to know that life can be dangerous and that infants are exceptionally vulnerable to the tragedies that can befall human beings and cut short their lives.

What a surprise it was to me, then—sometime in my college years—when I encountered the passage in Revelation from which the pastor had adopted the phrase, "the lamb's book of life." The verse refers to people who follow a beast that arises from the sea: "All the inhabitants of the earth will worship it, everyone whose name has not been written from the foundation of the world in the book of life of the Lamb that was slaughtered" (Rev. 13:8). The "lamb" in question is anything but the weak, gentle baby of my imagination. This "lamb" is the almighty, all-powerful Lamb to whom all nations will bow down.

The image of the Lamb is a marvelous example of how enriching figurative language can be. In the book of Revelation, the Lamb serves as a metaphor for Jesus Christ. Chapter 5 introduces this Lamb: "Then I saw . . . a Lamb standing as if it had been slaughtered" (5:6). The fact that the previous verse calls this personage "the Lion of the tribe of Judah" shows how different this Lamb is from a meek, sacrificial victim. This Lamb is victorious and conquering; he is supremely powerful. Not only does he make war on the kings and beast (12:14), but he also holds power over the physical universe as well. As chapter 6 portrays the curses of the sixth seal, whereby the sun is blackened, the moon is bloodied, and the stars fall out of the sky, the writer asserts that all of these disasters are due to the "wrath of the Lamb" (6:16).

Yet this Lamb is not only warlike and combative. The Lamb is also protective. Chapter 7 tells us about those dressed in white robes, for whom the Lamb that is "at the center of the throne will be their shepherd" (7:17). Likewise, chapter 21 likens the people of God to the "bride, the wife of the Lamb" (21:9). How rich all this imagery is! In ways that literal language cannot, figurative language expresses truths about reality and draws them close to our hearts.

> In allegory, the writer portrays persons, places, and events from the Old Testament as representing something relevant to New Testament times.

Figurative language has always played a part in understanding the scriptures. At the same time, such nonliteral interpretations have sometimes been seen as dangerous. Now and then, you may have heard a minister on television pronouncing forcefully, "I take the Bible literally." The irony is that the persons who make these kinds of statements do not really mean them literally. Otherwise, when they deal with the creation accounts in Genesis 1—3, for example, they would need to portray God as possessing a physical form. To take the account of the Garden of Eden in Genesis 3 completely literally, you would need to envision the Lord God as a being with arms and legs, for when Adam and Eve have eaten of the forbidden fruit, they become fearful as they hear God "walking in the Garden" (3:8). To reconcile such a literal understanding of the text with the familiar affirmation in John that "God is a Spirit" (John 4:24) would be difficult indeed.

This discussion may seem somewhat frivolous, but some groups, particularly the Mormons, do indeed take Genesis this literally. The issue becomes serious when we turn to the creation account in Genesis 1. There we read that God created the world in six days. Is this literal or figurative? Debates have raged over the proper understanding of this chapter, but we won't discuss it in detail here. Suffice it to say that many people wish to maintain a highly literal interpretation of the creation story, but the attempt to do so creates myriads of problems, even within the text itself.

Figurative interpretation, especially in the form of allegory, was a beloved practice in the early church. In a sense, allegory goes back to the apostle Paul himself. In the letter to the Galatians, Paul strives to show that the way of faith in Christ is the way of freedom. In contrast, the way of the law means bondage. To illustrate his case, he reaches back to the story of Sarah and Hagar in Genesis 16 and 21:

> For it is written that Abraham had two sons, one by a slave woman and the other by a free woman. One, the child of the slave, was born according to the flesh; the other, the child of the free woman, was born through the promise. Now this is an allegory: these women are two covenants. One woman, in fact, is Hagar, from Mount Sinai, bearing children for slavery. Now Hagar is Mount Sinai in Arabia and corresponds to the present Jerusalem, for she is in slavery with her children. But the other woman corresponds to the Jerusalem above; she is free, and she is our mother. (Gal. 4:22–26)

Do you catch the irony in this description? As understood by Paul's Jewish contemporaries, Sarah and her son Isaac initiated the line that carries God's covenantal promises, affirmed at Mount Sinai and culminating in the city of Jerusalem with its Temple. Hagar was Sarah's servant. Her son could thus be associated with slavery and was certainly not on the same level with Isaac.

Paul turns this around completely. He suggests that it is those who put their faith in Jesus Christ who possess true freedom. Therefore, they are really the "children of the promise, like Isaac" (4:28). It is they who are in Sarah's line, while those who put their trust in Sinai and Jerusalem now belong in the line of Hagar.

You can imagine how Paul's reversal of the normal understanding of the descendants of Abraham, Sarah, and Isaac would be received within Jewish, or Judaizing, circles. For our purposes here, I want to note one feature of this pattern of interpretation. Persons, places, and events from the Old Testament are portrayed as representing something related to the New Testament. Isaac becomes the figure for believers in Christ; Ishmael represents those who wish to require the law as part of faith in Christ. Hagar, as a mother, is identified with Jerusalem. "Allegory" is the name Paul gives to this manner of relating the old to the new covenant: "Now this is an allegory" (4:24).

In the time of the early church, and for centuries thereafter, allegory became a beloved method of interpretation. Church leaders such as Origen, Augustine, Ambrose, Jerome, and many others were captivated by the power of allegory to find hidden meanings in the scriptures of both Testaments. Origen, the great third-century Alexandrian theologian, was particularly influential in developing the theory of allegorical interpretation. He differentiated between three levels in scripture passages. The first was the literal, historical sense; the second a moral sense; and the third, an allegorical sense.[1] By the early Middle Ages, theologians had added a fourth category as well, one that dealt with the future hope of Christians.

For Origen and for most others, the literal sense held little interest. God's great truths had been cast in a literal form only in order to give simple believers—that is, those who could not understand the deeper levels of divine revelation—something they could hold on to for their faith. What was really significant, instead, were the higher levels of interpretation, where much more profound insights could be gained from the words of the text.

You may detect here a hint of an elitist attitude. Along with the disdain for literal interpretations, practitioners of allegorical interpretative methods were sometimes contemptuous of the common folk who were not trained in the art of finding deeper meanings in the text. This amounts to an assumption that there are two levels of Christians in the church, with one level being clearly superior to the other. As an aside, it is worth noting that this sort of distinction between two levels within the faith has appeared frequently in Christian history. Naturally, those who make this sort of distinction invariably place their own group on the higher level.

> The meaning of scripture is to be found preeminently in the "plain Word of God."

On the one hand, it is certainly true that allegory can provide rich insights into the meaning of the Bible. On the other hand, as you probably suspect, the number of possible meanings available within an allegorical approach is limited only by the imagination of the interpreter. This is why the Reformation objected so strenuously to the medieval church's use of scripture. The penchant for allegory had reached incredible heights. The Reformers insisted that steady, down-to-earth interpretation was more fitting to the nature of the scriptures than was the soaring, imaginative interpretation of medieval allegory. This is the reason for the assertion in the Westminster Confession: "the full sense" of any biblical text "is not manifold, but one."[2]

Let's return to Paul's comments in Galatians 4 for a moment. His depiction of Sarah and Hagar—which, as we saw, he calls an allegory—is different from the allegorical method of later centuries. He does not devalue the literal events, but rather uses them to illustrate points he wishes to make. To distinguish Paul's approach from the more defined allegorical method of the ancient and medieval church, his style of interpretation is often called *typology*. In passing, we might also note that, while Reformers such as Luther and Calvin rejected allegory, they were well aware of—and appreciative of—figurative elements in the scriptures.

Taken in a rather broad sense, typology is without doubt a favorite and frequent practice for many people. Everyone from laypersons in Bible study groups to ministers preparing sermons can and does use typological interpretation profitably.[3] A better term for this practice, however, would probably be *application*. Simply stated, the goal is to take a story or event from scripture as a pattern that has relevance for our lives in the present.

The "Plain Sense" of Scripture

When the Reformers repudiated the excesses of allegorical interpretation, they sometimes couched their response as an appeal to preserve the "plain sense" of scripture. What the "plain sense" means is manifest in a somewhat flowery statement from the Scots Confession of 1560: "If the interpretation or opinion of any theologian, Kirk [Church], or council, is contrary to the plain Word of God written in any other passage of Scripture, it is most certain that this is not the true understanding and meaning of the Holy Ghost, although councils, realms, and nations have approved and received it."[4]

The firmness and resolve in this statement echo Martin Luther's declarations of his adherence to scripture. The writers of this confession assert that the meaning of scripture is to be found preeminently in the "plain Word of God." Thus, even though an approved doctrine or interpretation is regarded as authoritative by the church or government entities, if it appears to stand in conflict with the scriptures, taken as a whole, it is to be rejected.

This may seem somewhat self-evident, but we should remember that in the context of the times, this was a radical idea indeed. The official teaching of the church declared that the authority of ecclesiastical interpretation supercedes all other understandings of the Bible. Already in one of Martin Luther's earliest writings, *An Appeal to the Ruling Class* (1520), he complained about the presumption that official church teaching alone was sufficient to guarantee its soundness. Luther asserted that "it is a wicked, base invention . . . to aver that it is the function of the pope alone to interpret Scripture, or to confirm any particular interpretation."[5]

By this point in history, the infallibility of the pope, as the successor to Peter, had become an established belief within the church at large. The formal doctrine of papal infallibility itself was not actually promulgated by the church until much later, in 1870, at the First Vatican Council. Nevertheless, the basic concept was already well established, and it held that the guarantee for truth resides in the authoritative hierarchy. On matters of doctrine and ethics, the church could not err, since it was guided by, and preserved by, the Holy Spirit across the ages.

Given that abuses were rampant on the eve of the Reformation and many people in the priesthood were uneducated, Luther could write with not a little sarcasm, "The Romanists profess to be the only interpreters of Scripture, even though they never learn anything contained in it their whole lives long."[6]

> Careful attention to scripture may require us to revise our understanding and interpretation of the gospel message.

Luther's sharp words remind me of a somewhat amusing incident in an admittedly much less serious situation. When I was in seminary, I attended a Sunday morning class in a local church as part of a field work assignment. At the time, the Presbyterian Church was in the midst of approving a *Book of Confessions* that would supplement adherence to the traditional Westminster Confession. Tensions around the proposed changes were running high. On that particular morning, a woman in the class made an impassioned plea to stick to the Westminster Confession because it was safer and better. Later in the class period, the teacher commented on Jesus' incarnate nature. When he affirmed that Jesus was both fully divine and fully human, the woman's hand shot up in the air. She insisted that such a view was impossible and a little irrational. The teacher could hardly restrain a chuckle as he pointed out that what he had said was precisely the position that the Westminster Confession professes.

This woman was defending the confession passionately, but she did not really know the content of the document very well. Sometimes the strongest advocates for a particular text—be it a confession of faith or the Bible itself—are not the most serious students of that text. At the beginning of the Reformation, Luther implied—somewhat sarcastically, as we saw—that some of those in the hierarchy who claimed that they were the only authoritative interpreters of the Bible did not read it frequently, if ever.

The Reformation's claim that scriptural interpretation ought not be subject to the hierarchy of the church did not go uncontested. As positions hardened and Christendom was dividing into competing bodies, the Catholic Church dealt with this issue at the long-running Council of Trent. In the decree on scripture, published in 1546 shortly after the council opened, the council declared that

> no one relying on his own judgment shall, in matters of faith and morals pertaining to the edification of Christian doctrine, distorting the Holy Scriptures in accordance with his own conceptions, presume to interpret them contrary to that sense which holy mother church, to whom it belongs to judge of their true sense and interpretation, has held and holds, or even contrary to the unanimous teaching of the Fathers.[7]

If you place this declaration beside the assertion in the Scots Confession quoted above, you will notice that there is a divergent assumption underlying each position. For the Council of Trent, it is not possible for the doctrine of the church to contradict the scriptures. On the surface, of course, the two may appear to be in conflict, but ultimately there will be no inconsistency between ecclesiastical doctrine and scriptural teaching. The Holy Spirit has been promised to the church to preserve it from error.

The Scots Confession, in contrast, assumes that there may truly be conflict between the teachings of the church and what is taught in the Bible. Not only *may* there be such conflict, but discrepancies *have in fact* marred the life of the church on many occasions. From the perspective of the Scots Confession, that is precisely the reason for the Reformation. Teachings on a whole range of issues—from papal authority, to indulgences, to the sacraments, to priestly celibacy, to justification by faith—had strayed from the understanding of Christian faith in the scriptures.

From the language used in these brief quotations, you can see how bitter was the split that developed some five centuries ago between Reformation churches and the Catholic Church. Thankfully, in the last half century, voices from both communities have moderated considerably. These days we have a much greater appreciation for each other's intentions to be faithful to Jesus Christ, and we recognize much better our mutual unity in the Christian faith. Nevertheless, the basic underlying assumptions have not changed greatly. For the Catholic Church, the teaching authority of the church remains unassailable because it comes with a guarantee of infallibility. For churches in the Reformation tradition, in contrast, careful attention to scripture may require us—and every other church—to revise our understanding and interpretation of the gospel message. These are diametrically opposed positions, and it will be a long time before a resolution will be found between them.

"The plain sense" of scripture that is so important to the Reformation has often been described with another phrase: "scripture as its own interpreter." The fundamental point is presented succinctly in the Westminster Confession: "The infallible rule of interpretation of Scripture, is the Scripture itself; and therefore, when there is a question about the true and full sense of any scripture (which is not manifold, but one), it may be searched and known by other places that speak more clearly."[8]

In the previous chapter, we dealt with the question of whether texts are "clear" or "unclear." Here I want to stress the part of this statement that asserts that biblical passages are to be understood in the first place in the light of other biblical passages. When something seems unclear or questionable, the first place to go—and the final place, for that matter—is the Bible itself. In other words, our interpretation needs to be grounded in the text.

We have already noted how this principle, dear to the heart of the Reformation, excludes appealing to an official interpretation by an authoritative teaching body, as promoted in the Catholic Church. Does the same principle apply to Reformation churches themselves? I believe that it may, though in a somewhat subtle way. On the one hand, churches in the Reformation tradition have their own heroes. Martin Luther and John Calvin were prolific writers. Sometimes their writings have served as unofficial authorities in discussions about

> To interpret or not to interpret is not the question. The question is rather to interpret well.

doctrinal issues or interpretations of biblical texts. Particularly in some of the smaller groups issuing from Protestantism, as we mentioned in the last chapter, the writings of founding leaders have occasionally been accorded nearly the same level of authority as the scriptures themselves.

There is another danger, in the context of our current use of study Bibles. Editions of the scriptures with study notes and reference materials are valuable. They can help to understand the meaning of the text much better than might otherwise be the case. Take a passage like the words of Jesus to the women of Jerusalem on his way to the cross. As he sees them wailing for him, Jesus says, "Daughters of Jerusalem, do not weep for me, but weep for yourselves and for your children. For the days are surely coming when they will say, 'Blessed are the barren, and the wombs that never bore, and the breasts that never nursed.' . . . For if they do this when the wood is green, what will happen when it is dry?" (Luke 23:28–31). When you read the last sentence about the green wood and the dry wood, you are likely to be puzzled. What does Jesus mean? A good study Bible will be a great source of aid in such a situation.

What, then, is the danger with study Bibles? Just this: Many people are tempted to assume that the notes in the Bible are equal in authority with the text. Somehow, the fact that the words—text and notes—are printed on the same page tends to identify them in people's minds, so that we can all too easily assume that they belong together. The result, however, is that we ascribe more authority to the notes and comments than is warranted. When we use a study Bible, we must remember that it is the text, not the notes, that is inspired. Or, to put it differently, when we speak of "scripture as its own interpreter," it is the text, not the notes, that must provide the authoritative interpretation.

Postmodern Interpretation

At the beginning of this chapter, we commented on the claim made by some people that we should always interpret the Bible strictly literally. We saw too that purely literal interpretation obviously misreads the basic intention of some biblical texts. At the other end of the spectrum, there is a current of thought in our day that argues that the interpretation of the text really comes down to the meaning that the reader assigns to it. Called *postmodernism,* this is an amorphous movement with many variations, rather than a tight theory. The general position holds that all writings of whatever kind have multiple meanings, depending on the setting and perspective of the persons who are reading a particular text.

This viewpoint advocates just the opposite of what those who insist on literal interpretation endorse. For postmodernism, the initial intention of an author of a text is not at all determinative for the meaning we find in that text. The original meaning may be decisive for the author, but it is not binding on us. A text has only the meaning that the current reader finds in it or attributes to it.

You can imagine what a radical shift this introduces into biblical interpretation. Instead of seeking to uncover the meaning intended by the author and striving to apply it in our context, we would simply move to the question of what this passage says to us at this moment in time. This may sound somewhat familiar, since readers of the Bible—either alone or in group studies—will often use a similar sort of procedure. They will approach a biblical text and ask the question, "What does this passage say to me?" There is, thus, a superficial similarity here between such Bible reading and postmodern interpretative theory. In fact, there is also an identical danger in each: Our understanding of the message God may intend for us in the context of this passage may readily become highly subjective—based much more on our feelings, needs, wants, or predilections than on anything very concrete in the text itself.

Nevertheless, there is a significant difference between these two approaches. In principle, Bible reading of the first type does intend to be founded on the original intention of the text. If readers of this sort were told that their understanding seemed to be quite different from, or perhaps in contradiction with, the seeming meaning of the author, these readers would likely consider rethinking the conclusions they had just drawn.

Postmodernism's position is different in principle. For this approach to interpretation, there is no objective meaning of the text to be discovered. You and I, as readers, give meaning to the passage we are reading. For a postmodern interpreter to be told that his or her reading varies greatly from the manifest meaning of the author is a matter of indifference. For the more radical of postmodern interpreters, it may even be taken as a badge of honor.

This is not the place to go into a detailed discussion of this philosophy of reading and interpretation. I am mentioning postmodernism here simply because of its generic popularity in modern culture.[9] From our previous discussions, it is probably obvious to you that this approach is profoundly different from the Reformation's notion of the plain sense of scripture.

Interpretation is unavoidable. Thus, to interpret or not to interpret is not the question. The question is rather to interpret well. The "plain sense" of the Reformation encourages us to strive to understand the scriptures in light of the original intentions of the authors. It encourages us to remember that scripture is its own best interpreter. Ultimately, the authority of the Bible for our lives is dependent on our interpreting its meaning accurately. In our final chapter, we will consider some specifics regarding how we can interpret the scriptures appropriately.

Questions for Reflection

- We have mentioned a number of examples of passages that have a figurative sense. Think of some more from different parts of the Bible. What meaning do you derive from them in a figurative sense? What would the passages look like if you tried to understand them literally?

- The Gospel of John is noted for offering double meanings in the words of Jesus and in the events of his life. Locate some of these in the Gospel and discuss their literal and symbolic meanings.

- How easily do you find that you can understand the scriptures? What ideas do you have for yourself and for others about becoming equipped to interpret the Bible well?

Chapter 7

Utilizing an Authoritative Scripture

*I*n the previous chapter, we looked at the question of interpretation. How we interpret the Bible is integrally related to its authority. In this final chapter, we will say a few words about the authority of scripture. Then we will address some practical considerations that will help us interpret scripture in concrete situations in ways that will be accurate and beneficial for our faith and life in Christ.

The Authority of Scripture

Virtually all Christian traditions hold that the Bible is authoritative for our lives as followers of Jesus Christ. Within the Reformed tradition, for example, the Second Helvetic Confession makes the point clearly. Its opening words are: "We believe and confess the canonical Scriptures of the holy prophets and apostles of both Testaments to be the true Word of God, and to have sufficient authority of themselves, not of men. For God himself spoke to the fathers, prophets, apostles, and still speaks to us through the Holy Scriptures."[1] The Confession of 1967 presents a similar picture of the place of the Bible in the church and in Christian lives: "The one sufficient revelation of God is Jesus Christ, the Word of God incarnate, to whom the Holy Spirit bears unique and authoritative witness through the Holy Scriptures, which are received and obeyed as the word of God written."[2]

> The statements "the scripture says" and "God says" are roughly identical.

In chapter 3, we considered the inspiration of the scriptures. The authority of the Bible flows directly from the affirmation of its inspired character. If the scriptures are, as the Second Helvetic Confession puts it, "the true Word of God," then to recognize that they possess authority follows automatically. It is important to note at the very beginning, however, that affirming the authority of the Bible does not imply that all things contained in it are authoritative.

90

The confessions of the church make it clear that authority deals with our beliefs and actions, our faith and life. Ponder these words of the Second Helvetic Confession, for example: "And in this Holy Scripture, the universal Church of Christ has the most complete exposition of all that pertains to a saving faith, and also to the framing of a life acceptable to God; and in this respect it is expressly commanded by God that nothing be either added to or taken from the same."[3]

The Confession of 1967 echoes this viewpoint when it proclaims that the Old and New Testaments offer the witness in which the church "hears the word of God and by which its faith and obedience are nourished and regulated."[4] We come to scripture, as these examples indicate, for authoritative guidance in two areas: faith and life. That is, the Bible enables us to know what to believe and how to live. It offers us insights and authoritative counsel on doctrine and ethics.

In attributing authority to the scriptures, we are simply following in the footsteps of the early church. When New Testament authors spoke of the Old Testament, they often identified its words with those of God. The statements "the scripture says" and "God says" are roughly identical. In a telling passage, Paul writes, "And the scripture, foreseeing that God would justify the Gentiles by faith, declared the gospel beforehand to Abraham, saying 'All the Gentiles shall be blessed in you'" (Gal. 3:8). If you trace this quotation back to its sources in Genesis 12:3 and 18:8, you will discover that the words are part of the blessing promised to Abraham. The speaker is God.

> "We believe that the Word contained in these books has proceeded from God, and receives its authority from him alone, and not from men." (French Confession of Faith, 1559)

Scripture bears divine authority in its very words. There is a fascinating account in Acts 23, where Paul is forced to defend himself before the council in Jerusalem. Luke records the high priest, Ananias, ordering Paul to be struck on the mouth. Paul responds with a stern rebuke: "God will strike you, you whitewashed wall! Are you sitting there to judge me according to the law, and yet in violation of the law you order me to be struck?" (Acts 23:3). Paul's language shifts abruptly, however, when he learns that the man he is facing is the high priest. "I did not realize, brothers, that he was high priest; for it is written, 'You shall not speak evil of a leader of your people.'" (v. 5). You can almost hear Paul adding, under his breath, "even though he deserves it!" The point, however, is that Paul acknowledges a scriptural command that is to be obeyed. The only words he needs to use in order to introduce the command are, "for it is written."

Thus, to say "it is written" is to quote an authoritative pronouncement that is expected to end any and all debate. I write "expected to" because, as you can imagine, people then as now could ask questions about precisely how a given biblical statement was intended: Should this statement be interpreted in this way, or could we perhaps interpret it in another way? Is that really what this verse means for us today, or can we understand it differently?

Before considering the significance of this for our own life in the present day, we should pause for a moment to notice an instructive incident in the life of Jesus. One of the earliest observations about Jesus in the Gospel of Mark is the remark: "They were astounded at his teaching, for he taught them as one having authority, and not as the scribes" (Mark 1:22). The scribes, or teachers of Israel, limited themselves to commenting on the Hebrew Scriptures. They attempted to elucidate the meaning of what was written, but the text always remained the final authority. With Jesus, however, the authoritative text might become the starting point for a further authoritative pronouncement. Recall the classic phraseology in the Sermon on the Mount in Matthew: "You have heard that it was said to those of ancient times, . . . But I say to you . . ."[5]

The words of Jesus carried the same weight for the early Christians as did Old Testament declarations. In practice, then, the words of the Old Testament—interpreted in the light of Jesus Christ—embodied undoubted authority for the early church. Still, disagreements could arise about what to believe and how to live. Much of the New Testament is written to deal with such issues.

In all of this, life in the current church resembles closely the experience of the earliest believers in Christ. In nearly all denominations today, the members agree that the Bible is our final authority. At the same time, there are remarkable divergences in Christian beliefs among the denominations, and often the differences are quite deep. Not only that, but even among members of the same faith traditions, disagreements and disputes are heated. Thus, it would appear that subscribing to the authority of the Bible in principle often does not go together with unanimity regarding what the Bible in fact teaches.

In light of our previous discussion of interpretation, it is probably obvious where the problem resides. Simply put, different people interpret the scriptures in different ways. Two interpreters may avow biblical authority in identical words, but their modes of interpretation may vary greatly.

On one level, interpreters may read given passages in the Bible in contrasting ways, and the result is not just divergences between one interpretation of a passage and another. Sometimes there are outright contradictions between them. To take an obvious example: Many people within the Protestant evangelical tradition read the book of Revelation, along with other prophetic books, in as literal a manner as possible. Consequently, they find in the text a rather precise blueprint for the final days of earth prior to the return of Christ. Others highlight the metaphorical language of the book of Revelation and conclude that we should not expect to find concrete information about dates and events in it, but rather symbolic presentations of the final victory of God and Christ over sin and evil.

On another—and deeper—level, interpreters sometimes come to the scriptures with differing assumptions or presuppositions. (There is usually an element of this hidden away in any major difference of interpretation.) Such differing assumptions will result in contrasting conclusions regarding the meaning of the biblical passages. Sometimes the divergent assumptions are obvious. To take an easy example, in the middle of the last century, Rudolf Bultmann wrote a little book called *Jesus Christ and Mythology*. He stated early on his assumption that modern people "take it for granted that the course of nature and of history, like their own inner life and their practical life, is nowhere interrupted by the intervention of supernatural powers."[6] Compare this forthrightly antisupernaturalistic presupposition with the starting point of someone who accepts the statements about Jesus Christ's virgin birth, resurrection, and ascension in the Nicene and Apostles' Creeds as historical, literal events. It is not difficult to forecast the different directions theirs and Bultmann's interpretations of an event like the stilling of the sea in Luke 7 would go!

At other times, the assumptions that underlie interpretation may be quite subtle. Within the Lutheran and Reformed traditions, for example, there is a significant difference with regard to what sorts of things are allowed in the life of the church, particularly in worship. For Luther, anything that is not expressly prohibited in the Bible is proper. For Calvin, in contrast, only those things that are specifically permitted are acceptable. The outcome, as you will be aware if you have visited Lutheran and Reformed churches, is a warmer, more "catholic" feel to the Lutheran sanctuary and a starker, even austere, sense in the Reformed sanctuary. Stained glass windows, pipe organs, statues, and art work: none of these are mentioned in the Bible per se. For Luther, therefore, they are permitted. For Calvin, they are prohibited.

Interpretation, then, is a key element in utilizing the scriptures. For the Bible to be truly authoritative in our day-to-day existence, for it to give us guidance for our faith and our life, we will have to interpret the Bible carefully and accurately. In addition, we will have to examine our own presuppositions, so that we recognize what viewpoints are appropriate and compatible with scripture and with life. In the remainder of this chapter, I want to suggest some procedures that can help ensure adequate interpretation of this book we call the Bible.

What's Your Canon?

In chapter 1, we noticed that there are slightly varying canons within the traditions of Christendom. To ask a question like "What is your canon?" is not to inquire about which of these various canons you adhere to or might prefer. The question intends instead to look at how we handle our own canon. I can illustrate the issue here with an incident that occurred to me some time ago when I overheard a seminary student discussing his plans for ministry after graduation. He was talking enthusiastically about serving a congregation and preaching weekly. One comment in particular struck me. It went something like this: "I hope to preach from the Old Testament now and then. It's interesting, especially the stories in it. But you know, I've hardly ever heard anyone preach on the books of the Old Testament."

> The phrase "a canon within the canon" describes the tendency to consider certain portions of the Bible to be more authoritative than others.

I will not try to gauge in these pages how accurately his comment may describe preaching in Protestant pulpits these days. But it does remind me of a second-century Christian named Marcion. He stressed radically the grace of God. He developed his own set of Pauline letters to support his position, excising material that suggested anything but grace. He rejected the Gospels too, apart from a strongly edited version of Luke. He also rejected the Old Testament wholesale, on the grounds that it presented a God of wrath. In effect, Marcion devised his own canon of scripture.[7]

Hardly anyone these days will pick and choose among the books that have come to be considered canonical in their tradition. Most people will claim that they believe the entire Bible to be authoritative. However, if people—for instance, pastors in their preaching ministry—hardly ever make use of the Old Testament, they would be moving dangerously close to Marcion. This is the sort of thing that I mean to raise with the question, "What is your canon?"

Any time we concentrate on certain parts of scripture to the exclusion of other parts—such as the New Testament or some part of it such as the Gospels or the Pauline letters —we are adopting what theologians have called a "canon within the canon." This expression indicates a tendency, either conscious or unconscious, to consider certain portions of the Bible to be more authoritative than others. The tendency has a long, well-established history.

Martin Luther can provide us with what is probably the best-known example of this kind of approach to the scriptures. Captivated by the doctrine of justification by grace through faith, Luther was disappointed to find a different sort of approach to faith and works in the letter of James. Luther concluded, therefore, that the letter is really "an epistle full of straw,"[8] not worthy to be ranked with the primary writings in the New Testament.

Probably all of us have a tendency to select a kind of canon within the canon. Whether we are preaching, developing classes in a church's educational ministry, or simply reading our Bibles, it is easy to be predisposed to prefer specific books. The same can happen readily as we return again and again to favorite passages and themes. These things are not problematic in themselves. The difficulty comes when one particular theme or one particular book is raised to a higher level than others. It is when we focus on one issue or concentrate on one theme in the Bible—proclaiming it to be *the gospel*—that we are in danger of selecting our own canon within the larger canon.

All through Christian history there has been a tendency in practice to adopt different canons. Often such choices are due to the predilections of individual interpreters or the preferences of a cultural period. Sometimes the reasons for certain choices are very specific. I have already mentioned Marcion in the early church, who wished to stress the absolute grace of God. For Martin Luther, as we saw, the favored theme

> All of us have a tendency to choose a "canon within the canon."

was justification by faith. Early in the twentieth century, the esteemed church historian Adolf von Harnack centered on "the simple gospel of Jesus." In the latter half of the century, the theological stream called liberation theology began to focus on passages, such as those in Exodus, that speak of escaping bondage and experiencing freedom.

More recently, the so-called Jesus Seminar has achieved notoriety in the media as well as in scholarly circles. Over the last twenty years or so, members of the Jesus Seminar have concentrated on the Gospels, with the intention of coming to some kind of consensus on what Jesus actually did and did not say and do. Members voted by color codes to determine the probabilities regarding the authenticity of the material. Four colors were used: red, pink, gray, and black, ranging from the indication that Jesus definitely did or said this (red), to the conclusion that Jesus definitely did not do or say this (black). The Seminar has been best known for its highly skeptical conclusions. Fifty percent of their votes were black, and another 30 percent were gray. Thus, only about 20 percent of the Gospel material is judged by them to derive from material that is likely authentic.

Members of the Jesus Seminar do not represent the mainstream of biblical scholarship; a large majority of scholars reject their work as overly skeptical and based on a priori presuppositions. For instance, the Seminar assumes that nothing supernatural happens in this world; God does not intervene in exceptional ways in the cosmos. Thus, claims about Jesus' virgin birth or bodily resurrection, not to mention his feeding of the multitudes or walking on water, are eliminated in advance. Likewise, prophetic predictions by Jesus regarding his own death or claims to divinity as the Messiah or Son of God must all have been attributed to Jesus following his death.

The Jesus Seminar has also been criticized for its conscious attempts to gain notoriety in the media. Injecting provocative statements into their work has assured members of publicity. Nevertheless, whether or not we agree with their approach and conclusions, on the whole their work is carried on in a serious and exacting way. Two of the best-known writings emanating from the Seminar are John Dominic Crossan's *The Historical Jesus: The Life of a Mediterranean Jewish Peasant* and Marcus Borg's *Meeting Jesus Again for the First Time*.[9] The fact that Crossan and Borg arrive at such different portraits of Jesus—a Palestinian peasant with a political bent versus a prophetic holy man—also casts doubt on their methods. Seminar members have frequently been criticized for bringing their own pictures of Jesus to their assessment of the (very few) texts that they consider to be authentic.

I mention the Jesus Seminar here as an example of a group that operates with a canon within the canon, but not because they focus on the Gospels per se. After all, scholars have to concentrate their professional work on specific portions of scripture. Rather, I mention them here because of the criticism of their work that we have just noted. Seminar members come to the Gospel texts with a priori choices as to what kind of material can and cannot be authentic. While they justly reproach fundamentalists for reading biblical texts simply at face value, they themselves go to the opposite extreme, concluding in advance of analyzing the Gospel texts what can or cannot be genuine. The result is that the Jesus Seminar falls into the trap of choosing its own canon—and a very limited one at that—within the grouping of canonical Gospels.

As I remarked above, all of us probably have a tendency to choose a canon within the canon. We may prefer certain central themes, we may be inclined to favor certain books over others, or we may have favorite passages that we continually turn to in reading the Bible. In each of these cases, we will find ourselves in the realm of a canon within the canon.

Sometimes highlighting passages or themes in the scriptures is important. At times, we need to shout a particular word or theme from the rooftops in order to call the church, and perhaps society at large, to recover something that has been lost or undervalued. The calls for equality and justice during the civil rights struggles in the mid-twentieth century are an obvious example of such a need.

Likewise, on a more personal level, there may be times when certain books and words from the scriptures speak to us in a special way. For example, if we struggle with doubts about our self-worth, it may help to return frequently to passages that proclaim God's acceptance and love for all the creatures God has made. Some of Jesus' parables come to mind immediately. At different periods of our lives, we may also find that some passages speak to us with special power and meaning.

Finding help in particular passages of the Bible for social issues or for personal concerns is certainly legitimate. It is a very valuable use of the scriptures. Only if we begin to see such passages as more authoritative than others do we run the risk of adopting a canon within the larger canon of the scriptures. As we strive to understand and interpret the Bible, it is essential to remember the entire witness of scripture—the whole canon.

> A better question than "What does the Bible say?" is the question, "What sorts of things does the Bible say?"

The canon in fact exhibits marked diversity. As Martin Luther noted, for instance, the material in the letter of James is quite dissimilar to what we find in the letters of Paul. However, rather than viewing James as Luther did—as an inferior text—a better approach would be to consider what we can learn from this letter's distinctive presentation of the gospel message. Within some circles, the usual question is, "What does the Bible say?" A more beneficial question would be, "What *sorts of things* does the Bible say?" It is precisely the diversity in the Bible than can lead us to deeper and fuller insights in God's words for our own situations and needs.

The wisest approach to the canon is to consider the whole of it. It is best to keep in mind the different parts of the Bible, the different styles of literature it contains, and the range of material across both Old and New Testaments. Doing this will enable us to interpret more effectively the meaning of the scriptures for our faith and life as followers of Jesus Christ. In fact, we will be best served if we focus especially on those parts of the canon that we are not inclined to read or to use. Likely we will find truths and insights that will broaden our vision and deepen our understanding of what faith calls for in our lives in the present and for the work of the church in the world.

Striving to embrace the whole canon rather than a canon within the canon will aid us in interpreting the scriptures more usefully. There are also additional principles that we can adopt that will help to ensure that the Bible functions constructively in the church. Let us turn to these principles in the final section of this chapter.

Guidelines for Interpretation of Scripture

In the early 1980s, each of the two predecessor denominations of the Presbyterian Church (U.S.A.) adopted reports on biblical authority and interpretation. Recently, these papers seem to have been rediscovered in the denomination.[10] This may be because they provide a starting point for more objective attempts at interpreting difficult and sometimes divisive issues in the Presbyterian Church. In the course of the reports, various guidelines are put forward as guides for interpretation. In one place, seven guidelines are listed together.[11] Taken together, these seven guidelines can provide us with substantial assistance as we attempt to understand the meaning of the Bible adequately for our lives today. The guidelines stress the following principles:

"Take Christ out of the Scriptures and what more will you find in them?" (Martin Luther)

1. *Jesus Christ, the Redeemer, as the center of scripture.* The core of our faith is built around Jesus Christ. The focus of the Bible in both Old and New Testaments is on Jesus Christ, who has effected redemption. It is thus his words and deeds that provide the central principle to interpret biblical passages.

2. *The plain text of scripture.* Interpretation of scripture needs to focus on the plain meaning of the text. This is really the topic we were discussing in the previous chapter, when we dealt with the "plain sense" of the Bible.

3. *The guidance of the Holy Spirit.* The point of this guideline is to stress the need to depend on the leading of the Holy Spirit, promised in John 14—16, to guide us into all truth as we strive to interpret and apply God's message in the present. It is important to bear in mind that this guideline is qualitatively different from the others. The other six involve reasoned judgments regarding the correct approach to and understanding of a given passage of scripture. This guideline speaks to the appropriate attitude for us to adopt in interpreting the Bible. It recommends an attitude of openness and honesty, coupled with sincerity and humility.

4. *The "rule of faith."* This guideline points us to the value of continuity with the community and with tradition, which we discussed in chapter 5. The "rule of faith" refers first of all to the doctrinal consensus of the church, reflected in the primary creeds of Christendom, and then, more broadly, to the teachings of the church on doctrine, ethics, and Christian practices that are

accepted generally and have been passed down through the centuries as the cumulative wisdom of the church.

5. *The "rule of love."* This guideline, mentioned in both the Scots Confession and the Second Helvetic Confession,[12] harks back to Jesus' dual commandment of love for God and love for others (Matt. 22:36–40). It is a reminder that every interpretation should bear in mind those who are in disagreement with us as well as all others who may be affected by our interpretations.

6. *Earnest study of scripture.* This guideline serves as a reminder that difficult issues will not be resolved easily. They will require diligent work and study. It fosters careful consideration of the background and cultural settings of biblical passages, as compared to the cultural contexts in which we, as interpreters, live in the present.

7. *The whole scripture.* We addressed this particular guideline in the previous section of this chapter when we explored the importance of taking the entire canon into account when we interpret scripture.

These seven guidelines cover the waterfront in terms of what we need to consider in understanding a biblical passage correctly. To see how each guideline has been used in a concrete situation in the Presbyterian Church (U.S.A.), you will want to consult *Reading the Bible and the Confessions* by Jack Rogers.[13] He examines specific disputes in the denomination—historically controversial issues such as the ordination of women and the question of slavery—to see how these guidelines have been employed to arrive at an appropriate resolution. As you may suspect from the title, Rogers's book illustrates these principles with respect to both the Bible and the confessions of the Presbyterian Church.

For any major controversy in the church, applying one or another of these guidelines may incline us in different directions. After all, if the weight of all these principles tended in one direction, there would probably not be any serious controversy. It may just be that some of our seemingly intractable conflicts in the church, as well as some of our doctrinal divergences, are due in large part to the fact that people have put primary emphasis on different guidelines. For instance, if you place all the stress on the fourth guideline, the rule of faith, you are likely to come out with a different conclusion than if you emphasize the sixth guideline, the importance of earnest study of the Bible in light of its cultural setting.

We can illustrate this point nicely with a quick glance at an issue that continues to create division among the major communions of Christendom: the ordination of women. Since the 1970s, it has been church law in the Presbyterian Church (U.S.A.) that, as a consequence of the equality of men and women in Jesus Christ, women may hold any and all offices within the denomination.

In *A Brief Statement of Faith*, adopted in 1991, the denomination raised this truth to confessional status: "The same Spirit who inspired the prophets and apostles, rules our faith and life in Christ through Scripture, engages us through the Word proclaimed, claims us in the waters of baptism, feeds us with the bread of life and the cup of salvation, and calls women and men to all ministries of the Church."[14]

Many other Protestant denominations, such as the United Methodist Church and the Evangelical Lutheran Church in America, agree that women have the right to be ordained and to hold office in the church. Nevertheless, for some Protestant denominations, such as some Baptist traditions and smaller groups of Presbyterians such as the Presbyterian Church in America and the Reformed Presbyterian Church, the ordination of women is not permissible. We can add to these the Roman Catholic Church and the various Orthodox bodies. When all these denominations are grouped together, something like 80 to 85 percent of Christendom—officially, at least—disapproves of ordaining women to church office.

These seven guidelines will not furnish easy solutions, but they can help us sift through troublesome and sometimes painful disputes.

Until recent times, no significant denominations in the church ordained women to office. Thus, those who oppose ordination of women currently might well appeal to guideline 4, the "rule of faith." They would also appeal to guideline 2, "the plain text of scripture," for there are a number of passages in the Bible that appear to run counter to ordination, such as 1 Timothy 2:11–12: "Let a woman learn in silence with full submission. I permit no woman to teach or to have authority over a man; she is to keep silent." Finally, opponents might appeal to guideline 7, "the whole Bible," as well, arguing that the entirety of the Old and New Testaments points toward restriction of official leadership positions to men.

Which guidelines would those who favor ordination of women be likely to highlight? Guideline 1, "Jesus Christ as the center," would certainly rank high on the list. The sense that part of the core of Jesus' message deals with equality of all before God would provide support for ordination. Likewise, guideline 5, "the rule of love," would offer support for the idea of treating all persons equally. Guideline 6, "earnest study," could also be drawn in, for it underlines the need to consider cultural factors in understanding the implications of biblical statements for the present world. It is interesting that advocates of women's ordination would probably appeal to guideline 7 too. While admitting that the scriptures do presuppose a patriarchal culture, it could be argued that the Bible records a gradual movement in the direction of the equality of men and women.

If you have been keeping track along the way, you will notice that I have mentioned six of the seven guidelines. The one that remains to be considered is number 3, "the guidance of the Holy Spirit." As you can guess, both sides would readily appeal to this particular guideline. Either they would argue that it supports the traditional interpretation as the will of the Spirit, or they would claim that a new interpretation is required because the fresh breezes of the Spirit are providing a new course for the church. As mentioned above, this particular guideline relates more to the cultivation of an attitude of openness than to the search for evidence supporting specific conclusions. That is, it does not offer specific direction but rather encourages an open mind and heart to listen for the leading of the Spirit in arriving at God's will for a given, and disputed, situation.

> "Scripture is the School of the Holy Spirit."
> (John Calvin)

From this cursory illustration, it will be clear that these seven guidelines do not offer a simple, direct avenue to agreement on disputed and divisive issues. The guidelines are too general for that—or perhaps it would be more accurate to say that many issues are too complex. The guidelines do not serve as a sort of seven-step program. When issues of Christian faith and living are at stake, there is no easy formula to sort out the issues and arrive at a unanimous and unquestioned position. When disagreements are deep, the probability is that, with most of the guidelines, various sides in the discussion will be able to draw different conclusions regarding the impact of the guidelines on the correct interpretation of the biblical material.

However, to say that these guidelines will not furnish us with easy solutions to difficult problems is not to say that they are valueless. The contrary is the case. These seven guidelines can help us sift through troublesome and sometimes painful disputes to arrive at a better understanding of what is central in a given debate. For the guidelines to be helpful, we will need to bear certain things in mind.

First, as noted above, certain of the guidelines will favor one side on a controversial topic, while others will favor the opposite side. Likewise, if we advocate something strongly—particularly if it involves a doctrinal stance or a moral principle—we tend to see everything as pointing toward our position on the issue. The result is that we easily overlook evidence that witnesses against our favored position. If the guidelines as a whole are going to be of help to us, however, we will need to note objectively where one or another guideline offers support to a position contrary to our own.

Second, we all have a tendency to choose some guidelines over others, giving them added weight in our deliberations. Some people, for example, strongly favor guideline 4. Maintaining traditions is important to them, and they see major changes to the status quo as running counter to "the wisdom of the ages." It is better to stay with the tried and the true than to risk upheaval and unforeseeable consequences that might be harmful or disastrous. Others take the opposite course, embracing gladly guideline 6. For them, the limitations of culture are the salient point. When current culture moves in a different direction from assumptions in biblical times, we should readily recognize the limitations of the biblical worldview and willingly adopt a new stance. Each of us, then, has a predilection for certain of the guidelines.

Third, as an outgrowth of the first two points, it is essential to consider what all of the guidelines taken together have to say about a given issue. The denominational report gives equal emphasis to each of them. For these guidelines to be truly valuable, it is necessary to use them intentionally and systematically. That is to say, we need to ask very deliberately, "What does *this* guideline have to say about the Bible's witness on this question?"

When we consider the light that each of the guidelines can shed on a given issue, we will discover evidence pointing in various directions. Then the question becomes one of assessing the relative weight that we ought to give to each of the points in favor of one or another position on the issue. As we look at the collective evidence provided by the guidelines, we will be in a better position to judge where, and to what, the Lord God is directing us.

> "The Bible tells us not how we should talk with God, but what God says to us."
> (Karl Barth)

As we face conflicts and disagreements in the church, these seven guidelines can provide an invaluable service. Oftentimes, in the midst of ecclesiastical debates, we are prone to simply make our points and argue for our positions without honestly and objectively examining all sides in the discussion. Consciously analyzing an issue in light of all seven of these guidelines, however, will enable us to get a more complete and well-rounded picture of the issue at hand. We will recognize much more precisely what the implications are of the scriptures for our life and practice in the contemporary world. Then we will be in a position to come to a more effective and satisfactory conclusion about the will of Jesus Christ for our faith and life in this particular situation.

In the early days of the church, Paul's success in bringing the Gentiles to faith in Jesus Christ was disturbing to Jewish Christians, who believed that the new Gentile converts should be required to adopt the Jewish law as well. The conflict became so serious that, as Acts 15 describes it, the apostles were forced to debate the issue openly in a meeting that has come to be called the Jerusalem Council. Acts 15 includes a record of this interesting debate, which continued until a generally acceptable resolution could be found. Even then, not all were happy with the results. The remainder of Acts, along with other passages in the New Testament, bears witness to the continuing tensions around the issue of Gentile participation in the gospel. Those tensions did not cease until, tragically, the second century, by which time Jewish people had virtually ceased to be a part of the church of Christ.

Ever since this first serious conflict, there have been disputes of various kinds in the life of the church. Unfortunately, the current situation in our own and other denominations does not suggest that such disputes will cease any time soon! Even though we affirm the authority of scripture with one another, and even though we proclaim our desire to do Christ's will, we too often find ourselves on opposite sides of complicated and extremely divisive issues. The temptation frequently is to demonize one another rather than to listen attentively to each other's concerns and viewpoints.

At such times, it would be wise to remember the seven guidelines we have just considered. If we use them collectively and carefully, they can be a true gift of God to us. They can help us to see through the thicket of problems and controversies to paths upon which we can walk steadily and follow God faithfully. Applying these guidelines conscientiously to biblical interpretation will not resolve all our difficulties, but it will help us to go forward, along the lines of the yearning expressed in the Confession of 1967:

> With an urgency born of this hope [in God's final kingdom], the church applies itself to present tasks and strives for a better world. It does not identify limited progress with the kingdom of God on earth, nor does it despair in the face of disappointment and defeat. In steadfast hope, the church looks beyond all partial achievement to the final triumph of God.[15]

Questions for Reflection

- What is your favorite book of the Bible? Why is it your favorite? Do you find yourself returning again and again to the same passages? Are there books of the Bible that you have never read? Why not?

- Do you think you or your congregation tend to adhere to a canon within the canon? If so, what is it, and why do you think you or your congregation do so? What can you do to avoid maintaining a canon within the canon?

- Choose a topic that is debated in your congregation or denomination. What might the seven guidelines offer by way of an analysis of the issues? How does the debate look when you apply them collectively to the issues?

Conclusion

A Trustworthy Book

*T*he Reformation, as you can infer from the previous chapters of this book, put great stock in the trustworthiness of the scriptures. The Bible is inspired by God, and it comes alive in our hearts by the power of the Spirit. The Bible is sufficient and clear, containing all that we need to know in order for Jesus Christ to bring us to salvation. Thus, it is a book we can trust. Anyone—young or old, male or female, rich or poor—can come to this book confident that it will not fail them. Its pages will provide words of life, and reading it expectantly will stir us to the depths of our souls.

The Goal of the Scriptures

Earlier I spoke about the scriptures having been given to us not to provide information about a variety of more or less interesting topics, such as science, history, and geography, but rather to offer us what we need for faith and life. The goal of the scriptures is to nourish our spiritual lives, the core of our being, so that our lives—at work and at play, with family and with friends—will reflect the grace and mercy of Christ Jesus himself.

"The Bible is my heaven on earth!"

In the study group for which I first developed the material in this book, I asked the question, "What is the Bible for you?" One person said, "It's my heaven on earth!" She went on to comment that the people in scripture are like her relatives, and it was as though members of her family tree had passed down the stories through the generations. Another person remarked that, "I read and pray to find out where I fit into the story of scripture." Still another said, "The Bible is our concrete link to God, our compass to help us find our way."

At times, the Bible may indeed serve as our compass. At other times, it may be more like a mirror, disclosing what we are like. It may show us how we have succeeded in living faithfully and well, serving God and our neighbors. It may also reveal that we need a course correction or two. Spiritual growth is not a case of simply growing and being all grown up forever afterward. Along the path of spiritual development, we may need to relearn lessons again and again. In one way or another, as we read the Bible, we will find ourselves there. The Bible, in other words, is a handbook for life. It offers us the "lamp to our feet" and the "light to our path" of which Psalm 119:105 speaks.

Certain of the statements about scripture in the Westminster Confession are quoted often in discussions about the Bible. One remark that is not quoted so frequently is this: " . . . that the Word of God dwelling plentifully in all, they may worship him in an acceptable manner, and, through patience and comfort of the Scriptures, may have hope."[1] The confidence expressed in the last phrase echoes the wording of Romans 15:4: "For whatever was written in former days was written for our instruction, so that by steadfastness and by the encouragement of the scriptures we might have hope."

Notice that the confidence and hope expressed here are based on faith in the promises of the Bible. These are promises of God, and they are therefore absolutely reliable. They are founded on the almighty power of the Lord. As one of the authors of the Westminster Confession, Edward Reynolds, put it, God "is altogether omnipotent to do what [God] has purposed or promised."[2] The Reformers were thinking of this kind of trust when they spoke of the trustworthiness of scripture. It is a confidence that allows us to trust what life will bring, or rather, to trust in the God who will guide us through whatever life may bring.

> "Our faith in Scripture increases and decreases with our trust in Christ."
> (H. Bavinck)

The trustworthiness of scripture resides ultimately in its central point, Jesus Christ. In the Gospel of John, Jesus asks his disciples, "Do you also wish to go away?" Jesus has seen the crowds diminishing and his backers dwindling, and he is beginning to wonder how long the closest disciples will remain. Peter however, responds, "Lord to whom can we go? You have the words of eternal life. We have come to believe and know that you are the Holy One of God" (John 6:67–69). We might paraphrase that to apply to the Bible: "To what else can we go? The scriptures contain the words of eternal life, for they point us to the Christ." It is thus our trust in Jesus Christ that leads us to believe that the scriptures are trustworthy.

The early twentieth-century Dutch theologian Herman Bavinck remarks, "Our faith in Scripture increases and decreases with our trust in Christ."[3] Bavinck connects this observation to the fact that the church is imperfect and human faith is limited and weak. The ardor of Christian life goes up and down, for it is always subject to doubt and temptation. We should not expect, therefore, that we will continually have a lively sense of the trustworthiness of scripture. Now and then, the inspiration of scripture may sound like an idle dream, the suggestion of the sufficiency and clarity of the Bible may provide little comfort, and the illumination of the Spirit may leave us with hearts strangely cold.

At such times, we may feel far from a living, trusting relation to the Lord of the scriptures. The distance may seem so great that we want to cry out with words like those a discouraged father addressed to Jesus, "I believe; help my unbelief!" (Mark 9:24). Bavinck's point is that such times will likely come, but they will also go again. It is a question of continuing on with scripture. The issue is to keep seeking the Christ who inhabits its pages, for as we do so, we will gradually find, as did the travelers on the road to Emmaus, our "hearts burning within us" (Luke 24:32).

A Final Thought

When all is said and done, only one thing remains. That one thing is simply *to read the Bible*. At the beginning of this book, I noted that for many people, the Bible is a holy book, but it is also an unopened book. Ultimately, our theories about inspiration and illumination, as well as our professions about the Bible's sufficiency and clarity and trustworthiness, mean little if we never or rarely read the book.

Earlier we spoke of a variety of concerns: proper interpretation, reading in context, watching for metaphorical language, noticing the focus of scripture, being aware of the cultural contexts, and the like. Here I want to remind you of something that is less complicated. In the last analysis, what is the best way

> "Dig deeply into Scripture, not to get esoteric knowledge, but as a means to know Jesus Christ."
> (Edward Reynolds)

to deal with the Bible? Just read it! Long-term exposure to the scriptures, by which the words and phrases and thought forms seep into our hearts, will enable us to understand what the Spirit says to us. It is as the wording of the Bible becomes familiar and comfortable, like a long-time friend, that we will be able to recognize what it says and sense what it means for us.

A humble, open, receptive attitude will make the scriptures shine in our hearts. This parallels what John Burgess calls for when he encourages a "piety of the Word":

> Only as we recover disciplines of reading Scripture as a sacramental word might we nurture a different set of dispositions toward Scripture, so that we might receive it as a living word, not merely as information or practical advice. If we would discover the Word that Scripture might hold for us today, each of us must now "take, and read" in this spirit of confidence and humility.[4]

Burgess recommends the cultivation of new habits in our reading of scripture. We would be wise, he says, to practice such things as reading scripture aloud, reading it together in community, reading it in context (more sequentially and in larger blocks of material), and returning to the practice of memorizing scripture.[5] Such practices will help us to live from the riches of the Bible and to use its pages not just for information but for transformation.[6]

Where shall we start? When Martin Luther translated the New Testament into German, he added introductions to many of the books in order to help orient readers to their contents. In his preface to the whole New Testament, Luther offered his own opinion that "the true kernel" of the New Testament, that is, the books that should be ranked most significant, include the Gospel of John, the Pauline epistles, and 1 Peter. Luther then proposed, "Every Christian would do well to read them first and most often, and, by daily perusal, make them as familiar as his daily bread."[7]

We might want to add to Luther's list a few additional books, such as Matthew and Luke in the New Testament, and Genesis, Exodus, Psalms, and Isaiah in the Old Testament. Obviously, in light of the previous chapter, we will need to avoid viewing these central books as a canon within the canon. Nevertheless, returning to them often in our reading will provide a rich reservoir for our spirits, and they will provide sustenance for a piety of the word in our lives.

"God is faithful," the apostle Paul writes in 1 Corinthians 1:9. That faithfulness is the foundation for the certainty that scripture, as the Word of this God, is trustworthy. God's faithfulness ensures that we can rely on the Bible in all the circumstances of life. We can trust in it completely and fully for everything we finally need. Thus, the scriptures are indeed absolutely trustworthy, for by the power of the Spirit illumining our hearts, the scriptures will conduct us into an ever-closer relationship with the One who is at their center—Jesus Christ.

Questions for Reflection

- When all is said and done, what does the Bible mean to you? Or, to put it another way, what is the Bible for you?

- Do you find the Bible to be a trustworthy book? Are there times when you have experienced a distance from Jesus Christ or a sense that—even when you were reading the Bible—it was a closed book for you? What advice can you offer others (and yourself!) in such situations?

- Describe in your own words what it means to say that Jesus Christ is the center of the Bible.

Notes

INTRODUCTION: A HOLY BOOK

1. H. Wheeler Robinson, *Inspiration and Revelation in the Old Testament* (Oxford: Oxford University Press, 1946), 170.

CHAPTER 1: HOW THE BIBLE CAME TOGETHER

1. See Harry Y. Gamble, *A History of Early Christian Texts* (New Haven, Conn.: Yale University Press, 1995), 49–66. For a general discussion of how books were made in antiquity, see Bruce M. Metzger, *The Text of the New Testament: Its Transmission, Corruption, and Restoration*, 3d ed. (New York: Oxford University Press, 1992), 3–35.

2. As a matter of fact, there is no one canon accepted by all branches of Christendom. All are in agreement on the New Testament books, but the Roman Catholic Church maintains a larger canon than most Protestant bodies, while the Orthodox canon is larger still.

3. A translation of the Muratorian Canon is provided in Bruce M. Metzger, *The Canon of the New Testament: Its Origin, Development, and Significance* (Oxford: Clarendon Press, 1987), 305–7. Metzger offers his assessment of this canon on pages 191–201.

4. Already by the time of the Reformation, doubts regarding the authorship of Hebrews had again surfaced. Martin Luther, to take but one example, offered Apollos (mentioned in Acts 18:24–19:1 and elsewhere) as the author. Many since then have agreed with this supposition. Other names have been suggested as well: Barnabas, Luke, Clement of Rome, or even Priscilla.

5. John Barton, *How the Bible Came to Be* (Louisville, Ky.: Westminster John Knox Press, 1997), 90. See his entire book for more detail on the topics covered in this chapter.

CHAPTER 2: HOW THE BIBLE CAME TO US

1. Ivan Illich, *In the Vineyard of the Text: A Commentary to Hugh's* Didascalicon. (Chicago: University of Chicago Press, 1993), 87. See St. Augustine, *Confessions,* trans. Henry Chadwick (Oxford University Press, 1991), 92–93.

2. Ibid., 86–88.

3. Ibid., 54–58.

4. Harry Y. Gamble, *A History of Early Christian Texts* (New Haven, Conn.: Yale University Press, 1995), 120.

CHAPTER 3: DIVINE WORDS AND HUMAN WORDS

1. Justin Martyr, First Apology 36, in *Early Christian Fathers*, ed. Cyril C. Richardson, (Library of Christian Classics 1 (Philadelphia: Westminster Press, 1953), 265.

2. See, for example, Romans 16:22, Galatians 6:11, and 1 Corinthians 16:21.

3. Schleiermacher's strong emphasis on religious experience pressed him to locate inspiration in the inner life, and thus it relates to the experience of the authors of scripture rather than to the text itself. See *The Christian Faith,* ed. H. R. Mackintosh and J. S. Stewart (Edinburgh: T. & T. Clark, 1928), 591–603.

4. Charles Hodge, *Systematic Theology*, vol. 1 (Grand Rapids: Wm. B. Eerdmans Publishing Co., 1965), 154.

5. Ibid., 170.

6. Ibid., 157.

7. Harold Lindsell, *The Battle for the Bible* (Grand Rapids: Zondervan Publishing House, 1976), 174–76.

8. Confession of 1967, I.C.2 (9.27).

9. Ibid., I.C.2 (9.29).

10. G. C. Berkouwer, *Holy Scripture,* trans. Jack B. Rogers, in Studies in Dogmatics (Grand Rapids: Wm. B. Eerdmans Publishing Co., 1975), 162–63.

CHAPTER 4: THE WITNESS OF THE SPIRIT

1. John Calvin, *Institutes of the Christian Religion*, Library of Christian Classics, ed. John T. McNeill, trans. Ford Lewis Battles (Philadelphia: Westminster Press, 1960), 1.7.4.

2. Ibid, 3.1.4.

3. Second Helvetic Confession, I (5.002).

4. Ibid., I (5.005).

5. Westminster Confession, I.6 (6.006).

6. St. Augustine, *Confessions*, trans. Henry Chadwick (Oxford: Oxford University Press, 1991), 152–53.

7. From Pascal's "Memorial," written on the night of November 23–24, 1654. In Blaise Pascal, *Pensees*, ed. Louis Lafuma, trans. John Warrington (London: J. M. Dent & Sons, 1960), 203.

8. See also Proverbs 3:34 and Job 22:29.

9. Martin Luther, quoted in Paul Althaus, *The Theology of Martin Luther*, trans. Robert C. Schultz (Philadelphia: Fortress Press, 1966), 38n13.

10. G. C. Berkouwer, *Holy Scripture,* trans. Jack B. Rogers, in *Studies in Dogmatics* (Grand Rapids: Wm. B. Eerdmans Publishing Co., 1975), 41.

11. Westminster Confession, I.5 (6.005).

12. Ibid.

CHAPTER 5: SUFFICIENCY AND CLARITY

1. Westminster Confession, I.6 (6.006).

2. Martin Luther, quoted in Roland H. Bainton, *Christianity* (Boston: Houghton Mifflin Co., 1992), 250.

3. *Canons and Decrees of the Council of Trent,* trans. H. J. Schroeder (London: B. Herder Book Co., 1941), 17.

4. *Dei Verbum,* 2.9, in *The Documents of Vatican II* (New York: Guild Press, 1966), 117.

5. Raymond F. Collins, *First Corinthians*, vol. 7, Sacra Pagina Series (Collegeville, Minn.: Liturgical Press, 1999), 534.

6. Marjorie J. Thompson, *Soul Feast: An Invitation to the Christian Spiritual Life* (Louisville, Ky.: Westminster John Knox Press, 1995), 13.

7. "The Theological Declaration of Barmen," I (8.04).

8. Ibid., II.1 (8.11).

9. Ibid., II.2 (8.15).

10. The text of the Marburg Colloquy can be found in Donald J. Ziegler, ed., *Great Debates of the Reformation* (New York: Random House, 1969), 71–107.

11. *Dei Verbum,* 6.22, in *Documents of Vatican II,* 125.

12. Ibid., 6.25, in *Documents of Vatican II,* 128.

13. Westminster Confession, I.9 (6.009).

14. G. C. Berkouwer, *Holy Scripture,* trans. Jack B. Rogers, in Studies in Dogmatics (Grand Rapids: Wm. B. Eerdmans Publishing Co., 1975), 288.

15. Ibid., 298.

CHAPTER 6: DO YOU UNDERSTAND WHAT YOU ARE READING?

1. Origen, *On First Principles,* trans. G. W. Butterworth (New York: Harper & Row, 1966), 275–76.

2. Westminster Confession, I.9 (6.009). See Jack Bartlett Rogers, *Scripture in the Westminster Confession: A Problem of Historical Interpretation for American Presbyterianism* (Grand Rapids: Wm. B. Eerdmans Publishing Co., 1967), 414–45.

3. See Moises Silva, *Has the Church Misread the Bible?* (Grand Rapids: Zondervan Publishing House, 1987), 63–69. Silva offers a sympathetic account of the allegorical method, particularly in relation to Origen (see pp. 58ff.).

4. Scots Confession, XIX (3.19).

5. Martin Luther, "An Appeal to the Ruling Class," in *Martin Luther: Selections from His Writings*, ed. John Dillenberger (Garden City, N.Y.: Doubleday, 1961), 413.

6. Ibid., 412.

7. *Canons and Decrees of the Council of Trent*, trans. H. J. Schroeder (London: B. Herder Book Co., 1941), 18–19.

8. Westminster Confession, I.9 (6.009). "Scripture as its own interpreter" was sometimes called "the analogy of faith," a phrase taken from the language of Romans 12:6. See Rogers, *Scripture in the Westminster Confession,* 406–23.

9. For an excellent introduction to the values and implications of postmodern interpretation for biblical study, see A. K. M. Adam, *What Is Postmodern Biblical Criticism?* (Minneapolis: Fortress Press, 1995).

CHAPTER 7: UTILIZING AN AUTHORITATIVE SCRIPTURE

1. Second Helvetic Confession, I (5.001).

2. Confession of 1967, I.C.2 (9.27).

3. Second Helvetic Confession, I (5.002).

4. Confession of 1967, I.C.2 (9.27).

5. Matthew 5:21, 27, 31, 33, 38, 43.

6. Rudolf Bultmann, *Jesus Christ and Mythology* (London: SCM Press, 1958), 16.

7. It is often assumed that it was largely—or at least partially—in reaction to Marcion that the Orthodox Church began to develop its own canon more clearly.

8. Martin Luther, "Preface to the New Testament," in *Martin Luther: Selections from His Writings*, ed. John Dillenberger (Garden City, N.Y.: Doubleday, 1961), 19.

9. John Dominic Crossan, *The Historical Jesus: The Life of a Mediterranean Jewish Peasant* (San Francisco: HarperSanFrancisco, 1991); Marcus J. Borg, *Meeting Jesus Again for the First Time* (San Francisco: HarperSanFrancisco, 1994).

10. "Presbyterian Understanding and Use of Holy Scripture" and "Biblical Authority and Interpretation" (Office of the General Assembly, Presbyterian Church [U.S.A.], 1992).

11. "Biblical Authority," 52–53.

12. Scots Confession, XVIII (3.18); Second Helvetic Confession, II (5.010).

13. Jack Rogers, *Reading the Bible and the Confessions: The Presbyterian Way* (Louisville, Ky.: Geneva Press, 1999).

14. *A Brief Statement of Faith,* lines 58–64 (10.4).

15. Confession of 1967, III (9.55).

CONCLUSION: A TRUSTWORTHY BOOK

1. Westminster Confession, I.8 (6.008). For more on the meaning of this passage, see Jack Bartlett Rogers, *Scripture in the Westminster Confession: A Problem of Historical Interpretation for American Presbyterianism* (Grand Rapids: Wm. B. Eerdmans Publishing Co., 1967), 401–3.

2. Quoted in Rogers, *Scripture in the Westminster Confession,* 401.

3. Herman Bavinck, *Gereformeerde Dogmatiek* (Kampen: J. H. Kok, 1928), 1.569.

4. John P. Burgess, *Why Scripture Matters: Reading the Bible in a Time of Church Conflict* (Louisville, Ky.: Westminster John Knox Press, 1998), 142.

5. Ibid., 58–78.

6. On this theme, see M. Robert Mulholland, Jr., *Shaped by the Word: The Power of Scripture in Spiritual Formation* (Nashville: Upper Room, 1985).

7. Martin Luther, "Preface to the New Testament," in *Martin Luther: Selections from His Writings*, ed. John Dillenberger (Garden City, N.Y.: Doubleday, 1961), 18.

For Further Reading

Achtemeier, Paul J. *Inspiration and Authority: Nature and Function of Christian Scripture.* Peabody, Mass.: Hendrickson Publishers, 1999.

Adam, A. K. M. *What Is Postmodern Biblical Criticism?* Minneapolis: Fortress Press, 1995.

Barr, James. *The Bible in the Modern World.* Philadelphia: Trinity Press International, 1990.

Barton, John. *Holy Writings, Sacred Text: The Canon in Early Christianity.* Louisville, Ky.: Westminster John Knox Press, 1997.

———. *How the Bible Came to Be.* Louisville, Ky.: Westminster John Knox Press, 1997.

Berkouwer, G. C. *Holy Scripture.* Translated by Jack B. Rogers. Grand Rapids: Wm. B. Eerdmans Publishing Co., 1975.

Braaten, Carl E., and Robert W. Jenson, eds. *Reclaiming the Bible for the Church.* Grand Rapids: Wm. B. Eerdmans Publishing Co., 1995.

Burgess, John. *Why Scripture Matters: Reading the Bible in a Time of Church Conflict.* Louisville, Ky.: Westminster John Knox Press, 1998.

Davison, James E. *The Bible Book of the Month.* Louisville, Ky.: Bridge Resources, 2000.

———. *The Year of the Bible* (*Manual* and *Participant's Book*), Louisville, Ky.: Bridge Resources, 1996.

Gamble, Harry Y. *A History of Early Christian Texts.* New Haven, Conn.: Yale University Press, 1995.

Greenlee, J. Harold. *Introduction to New Testament Textual Criticism.* Peabody, Mass.: Hendrickson Publishers, 1995.

Mulholland, M. Robert, Jr. *Shaped by the Word: The Power of Scripture in Spiritual Formation.* Nashville: Upper Room, 1985.

"Presbyterian Understanding and Use of Holy Scripture" and "Biblical Authority and Interpretation." Lousiville, Ky.: Office of the General Assembly, Presbyterian Church (U.S.A.), 1992.

Rogers, Jack. *Reading the Bible and the Confessions: The Presbyterian Way.* Louisville, Ky.: Geneva Press, 1999.

Silva, Moises. *Has the Church Misread the Bible? The History of Interpretation in the Light of Current Issues.* Grand Rapids: Zondervan Publishing House, 1987.

Smart, James D. *The Strange Silence of the Bible in the Church: A Study in Hermeneutics.* Philadelphia: Westminster Press, 1970.

Vawter, Bruce. *Biblical Inspiration.* Philadelphia: Westminster Press, 1972.